W9-BCK-731

"*Live Smart* is a conversational book packed full of wit and wisdom for younger readers. Buy it for the students you care about. It might contribute to the kinds of conversations that change the very trajectory of their lives."

—Dan DeWitt, Dean of Boyce College,
author of *Christ or Chaos*

"We all need godly wise counselors in our lives to point the way to the most God-glorifying path. *Live Smart* serves as that voice, giving clear direction for the journey you are beginning. Listen intently, learn deeply, love strongly, and live godly. You only have one life to live, live to the glory of God with all your might!"

—Steven J. Lawson, President, OnePassion Ministries,
Dallas, TX

"From the beginning, I've had a front-row seat to Dan's conversion and intentional walk with Christ. Dan's unrelenting desire has been to live purposefully and to make consistently wise choices. This book encapsulates his life story.

"*Live Smart* is worth every minute of reading and studying as you seek to live an intentional, gospel-centered life."

—Tom Mallard, Dan's mentor after conversion

"Dan Dumas underestimates the target audience of *Live Smart*. Yes, it is helpful for teenagers and young adults, but it is wise, biblical counsel for anyone seeking to live a life for God's glory— and for those seeking to influence others to do the same. I wish Dumas had written this book, and given it to me, years ago."

—Jason Allen, President of Midwestern Baptist
Theological Seminary & College

"Swipe, tap, or click and you find thousands of fresh voices telling you how to navigate through life. I don't recommend taking cues from overnight sensations, no matter how many likes they have. I prefer faithful voices who have been successful over the years. Dan Dumas is a time-tested preparedness specialist! In *Live Smart*, Dumas imparts seasoned insights as to what needs to be in our mental and spiritual backpacks, not just to survive, but to thrive!"

—Tony Nolan, Evangelist

"*Live Smart* is a great guide for anyone who wants to discover what it means to really follow Jesus. Every young Christian needs to read Dan's book!"

—Russ Lee, Singer/Songwriter for the group NewSong

"Dan Dumas is an organizational genius, brimming with wisdom and creativity. I have often sought counsel from him about practical leadership questions in my own life. Now we have a book that makes such counsel available to anyone. This book will help you get your life together and will inspire you to get out of whatever rut you find yourself in with understandable steps of how to proceed. I commend this book to everyone from the stressed corporate executive to the college student seeking to plan out his or her life."

—Russell Moore, President, Ethics & Religious Liberty
Commission of the Southern Baptist Convention

"*Live Smart* is like a Swiss Army Knife for life. It includes just about everything you need for living a life of intentionality without regrets. I am amazed by how much wisdom is packed into these pages, and I wish I'd had this tool when I was a young man. Dan Dumas is one of the most deliberate men I know, and this book mines his experience, wisdom, and knowledge of God's Word for truly living smart."

—Rick Holland, Pastor, Mission Road Bible Church,
Kansas City

LIVE SMART

Preparing for the Future
God Wants for You

DAN DUMAS

BETHANYHOUSE
a division of Baker Publishing Group
Minneapolis, Minnesota

© 2016 by Dan Dumas

Published by Bethany House Publishers
11400 Hampshire Avenue South
Bloomington, Minnesota 55438
www.bethanyhouse.com

Bethany House Publishers is a division of
Baker Publishing Group, Grand Rapids, Michigan

ISBN 978-0-7642-1776-0

Printed in the United States of America

All rights reserved. No part of this publication may be reproduced, stored in a retrieval system, or transmitted in any form or by any means—for example, electronic, photocopy, recording—without the prior written permission of the publisher. The only exception is brief quotations in printed reviews.

Library of Congress Control Number: 2015957337

Unless otherwise noted, Scripture quotations are from The Holy Bible, English Standard Version® (ESV®), copyright © 2001 by Crossway, a publishing ministry of Good News Publishers. Used by permission. All rights reserved. ESV Text Edition: 2007

Scripture quotations marked NASB are from the New American Standard Bible®, copyright © 1960, 1962, 1963, 1968, 1971, 1972, 1973, 1975, 1977, 1995 by The Lockman Foundation. Used by permission.

Cover design by Darren Welch Design

Author is represented by Wolgemuth & Associates.

17 18 19 20 21 22   8 7 6 5 4 3

In keeping with biblical principles of creation stewardship, Baker Publishing Group advocates the responsible use of our natural resources. As a member of the Green Press Initiative, our company uses recycled paper when possible. The text paper of this book is composed in part of post-consumer waste.

green
press
INITIATIVE

Dedicated to
my beloved sons, Aidan and Elijah,
future intentional leaders

Contents

Foreword

What difference can a book make?

When I was a teenager, a wise older friend put it to me straight: "At the end of the day, much of who you are will be decided by the people you know and the books you read."

This is a book that can make a real difference in your life, right now. Dan Dumas is a man who wants to make an impact in the world with his life, and he wants to help you to make an impact as well.

Where does it all start? Well, for the Christian, it all begins with seeking wisdom. This was King Solomon's great desire, and it should be ours as well. When Solomon asked God for wisdom, God gave it. We have much of the wisdom God gave to Solomon in the book of Proverbs, right in the middle of the Bible. Right after the Psalms, is a book all about wisdom.

Live Smart takes you through the wisdom God gave to Solomon, summarized into fourteen timeless principles for life—the kind of life that makes a difference in the world, and the kind of life that pleases God.

The greatest tragedy that can happen to any of us is to miss out on God's plan for our life. In this book, Dan Dumas walks you through these fourteen principles and shows how each principle can be real in your own life. Powerfully real.

When I read a book, I want to have confidence that the author knows what he is talking about. Dan Dumas is the right man to write this book. He is a leader and he is a man who helps others lead. He wants you to be a leader as well, and he wants you to live out God's plan for your life to its fullest.

Live Smart will make a difference in your life. You will really like how Dan Dumas writes about his own experiences gaining wisdom, and they were often painful lessons. He makes every one of these principles come to life, and he grounds every principle in the perfect wisdom of the Bible.

I never had the opportunity to know King Solomon. I missed him by about 3,000 years. Dan Dumas, on the other hand, I know very well. I know him as a committed Christian and I get to watch him as a man of character, a powerful leader, a teacher, a husband, a father, and a man of boundless energy. More than that, I know him as a friend. When you read this book, you will see why I am so thankful for this friend.

Read this book and mark it up. Underline what seems most important and pray about what you read. Be determined to make a difference for Christ and be determined to start right now.

Read smart. Be smart. *Live Smart*—all to the glory of God.

R. Albert Mohler Jr.
December 22, 2015

Acknowledgments

First and foremost, I want to thank my wife, Jane. She is patient, kind, and unconditionally loving toward me. Our forever love is what keeps me going. The way she lives the Christian life and the hard work she puts into raising our boys shine as an example and inspiration to me. Aidan and Elijah, my boys and our future, thank you for patiently listening to me work these truths out in our everyday lives. I pray they will find a home in your character and leadership.

I am deeply indebted to Matt and Anna Damico. Anna served as my executive assistant at The Southern Baptist Theological Seminary, and helped me champion Christ's hospitality and excellence on the campus. I want to express special gratitude to Matt, who is an especially gifted thinker and writer. Matt's prose, collaboration, and precision made this book possible. You are unmatched in helping me set the tone for this book. I am forever indebted to the countless hours and zeal you put into this project. You are an amazing servant of the King.

I am so thankful for my executive team, Charles (C.T.) Eldridge and Rachel Hunter, who are two of the finest leaders and servants of Christ. They continually make my life simple by handling all the logistics and strategy of our office, and have been especially instrumental in seeing this project to the finish line.

I am grateful for my VP Team at Southern Seminary. They are indomitable: full of ideas, always thinking outside the box, world-class leaders, and doing all of this while they love the church and raise children. With the aid of Christ, together we strive to raise the next generation of gospel leaders.

My team at Wolgemuth & Associates and my editing team at Baker/Bethany House, Andy McGuire, Jessica Barnes, Nancy Renich, thank you.

Finally, I am thankful for all my past and present mentors. God has been so generous to grant so many godly men throughout my life, who have shaped who I am today. I am especially thankful for Tommy Mallard, John F. MacArthur, a bazillion best friends, ministry co-laborers, elders past and present, and the executive team (past and present) at Southern Seminary. Last, but certainly not least, R. Albert Mohler, who exemplifies what it means to lead with intentionality at an early age, having taken the helm at Southern Seminary at age thirty-three. You, sir, had the conviction and relentlessness to lead Southern Seminary faithfully home.

July 2015
Louisville, Kentucky

Introduction

A Bear, a Lion, and You

The lion . . . is mighty among beasts and does not retreat before any.

Proverbs 30:30 NASB

A Bear

It was a crisp fall morning in the mountains of Idaho. I was on a guided elk hunt with friends. As the sun came up, we started calling for the elk and expected to see a bull elk in a matter of minutes. As I was getting my gear ready, I was interrupted by a noise behind me. Something was crashing through the woods. *Must be a small elk,* I thought. I made eye contact with my guide, and he gestured to me to take a look. I looked, and before long, my eyes were locked with a bear. I saw him and he saw me. He was unfazed by my presence and continued to march toward me. He was closing the gap.

My guide instructed me to jump out and make myself look big, in hopes of scaring off the bear. I jumped out, and at the same time realized that I didn't have my bow ready. My bear spray and pistol were in my backpack. I was totally unprepared for this encounter. The bear charged and growled. I stood my ground. Out of the corner of my eye, I saw that my guide had drawn his pistol and was running toward the bear. I decided I'd try to protect myself, hope my guide would shoot the bear, and hopefully I'd just get scraped up and maybe make the evening news. Fortunately for me, the bear got spooked ten feet away when he saw the guide charging, and he darted back into the woods. In camp that night they called me "the bear whisperer," and I now had a killer story. And I had learned a crucial lesson: Be prepared.

A Lion

Benaiah was a man who was more prepared for his encounter with the wild. He faced impossible odds, a bitterly cold day, snow on the ground, and a fierce predator.

> Benaiah the son of Jehoiada was a valiant man of Kabzeel, a doer of great deeds. He struck down two heroes of Moab. He also went down and struck down a lion in a pit on a day when snow had fallen.
>
> 1 Chronicles 11:22

This obscure but mighty text shapes the book in your hands. Benaiah didn't receive much press in the Old Testament, but his actions here are Herculean, his example stellar, and his story is worth a closer look.

I'm confident Benaiah didn't hesitate to jump into that snowy pit. He had trained himself for that moment by making a habit of doing hard things. When he stumbled on that abandoned pit and discovered a ferocious lion, his cold, numb hands clasped his sword with all his might, striking down the king of the jungle. The odds were against him, but that's just what leaders are built for. They do challenging things at inconvenient times and in inconvenient places.

You

Before you ever jump into a pit to slay a lion, or meet a bear in the woods, there are some things you need. You've got to have the right tools and materials. You may have all kinds of opportunities to jump into a pit and fight a lion, but only the prepared survive. Having the right tools, the right plans, and enough resources is required for anyone bold enough to engage in a life full of battles, lions, and bears. This is precisely why you need this book—so that you will have the tools you need to live smart.

I'll bet I'm older than you. I'm fifty, and I'm guessing you're not. When I consider the path of my life, there are things I'm proud of and things I would do differently, if I had the chance. There are times when I was ill-prepared for the challenges in front of me. I can only wish I would have had someone sit me down and give me some much-needed wisdom, some spiritual street smarts.

My singular goal in this book is to give you some of the guidance I missed as a young man. I want to pass on wisdom that I've learned from Scripture and from life, wisdom that I hope will save you from regrets. We're going to explore the paths God has created for us to walk in. I've walked a little further down those paths, and I want you to know that those roads are the way to a full, bold, intentional life that counts for eternity.

You are young and, Lord willing, have many decades still ahead of you. I want you to build a life that counts for eternity. You only get one life to live, and you can't leave it to chance. Get wisdom while you're young, and build a life that matters.

Part One

You + God

1

Fear God

The fear of the LORD is the beginning of wisdom,
and the knowledge of the Holy One is insight.

Proverbs 9:10

Have you ever stopped to think about what you want on your tombstone? I don't mean your frozen pizza, I mean your grave. When your friends talk about you at your funeral, what will they say? "John Smith was a really fun guy." Or, "Bill Jackson was fearless." There are definitely some things you don't want said, like "Susan Jones . . . was a fool."

The things you and I leave behind when we die—our legacy—is massively important. The way we can be sure people say good things about us when we're gone is to be intentional about the life we live in the present.

But beware: Living too much for the praise of others can be a trap. A snare.[1] Sure, it'll be nice for people to share a few kind words about us at our funeral, but you and I should be more concerned with the way we live before God right now. His opinion matters. He gets the last word. If God will say to us, "Well done, good and faithful servant," then who cares what other people think, right? Pastor Adrian Rogers said, "If you please God, it doesn't matter whom you displease; if you displease God, it doesn't matter whom you please." He's exactly right.

This truth hit me hard when I found myself in Cave Hill Cemetery in Louisville, Kentucky. I serve at a seminary in Louisville, and Cave Hill is home to the graves of some of the seminary's founders. I decided one day to wander over there, sit on a bench, and figure out what I want my epitaph to say. Sitting there that day, I understood something more deeply than I had before: One hundred percent of the world's population dies. Even these great men, whose lives left such huge impacts, died. I'm going to die someday. If I want my epitaph to say something good and true about me, I'd better get busy living right and honoring God in this life.

So let's say that because you're reading this book, you want to honor God with your life, too. If you do, there's an important first step. Ready? In order to live a life that pleases God, you've got to get wise. Not just smart. Not just clever. *Wise.* And all true wisdom flows from the same fountain: the fear of God.

This is why King Solomon, the wisest man to live before Jesus, wrote these words: "The fear of the LORD is the beginning of wisdom."[2] Earlier in his book of Proverbs, he wrote, "The fear of the LORD is the beginning of knowledge; fools despise wisdom and instruction."[3]

If that was true for King Solomon, then it's true for you and me.

Fear God Rightly by Knowing Him Truly

To live wisely means to fear God. Now, maybe you're asking yourself, "What does it mean to fear God?" Great question. It's not the kind of fear that a prisoner has for a harsh taskmaster who makes him want to run and cower. No, it's the kind of fear that a child should have for his or her father. You don't run away when your dad walks in, but you might sit up a little straighter. It's respect. It's reverence. It's recognition of who God is.

Imagine coming to the foot of Mount Everest, the tallest peak in the world. As you're getting ready to climb, your guide gives you some last-minute instructions. I'll bet you would listen to those instructions as intently as you've listened to anything in your entire life. Why? Because you have a healthy respect and fear for the task in front of you. You're not about to ascend a bunny hill. This is the highest mountain on Earth. You listen and you follow instructions because this mountain is bigger than you, and you do not want to take a wrong step.

So it is with God. You've got to recognize who he is. In other words, you've got to know him truly. You need a right view *of* God in order to live rightly *for* God. If you don't know him, you won't know how to live this life he gives us.

A good way to diagnose your view of God is to look at your daily life. If you have a high view of God, you will live with high standards; if you have a low view of God, you will live with low standards. If you've got a high view of God, your problems will seem small. If you've got a low view of God, your problems will overwhelm you.

At the center of every future gospel leader is a robust, right, and lofty view of God. A high view of God will produce a healthy fear of God and will inject zip and zest and zeal into your walk with God.

How do you cultivate a high view of God as a young man or woman? Learn some theology! *Theology* might seem like a big word that boring people talk about, but it simply means "the study of God." You'll only know someone if you study them. And believe me, theology is far from boring. If you think theology is boring, you're doing it wrong. God is the most fascinating and interesting subject and person you could ever study. Reading good and strong theology will help you understand just how incredible God is.

The most trustworthy source to learn about God is God himself, which means the best place to find good theology is right inside your Bible. Let's start by ransacking Psalm 139. This might scare you. These twelve verses have been the single greatest aid to my own personal sanctification (sanctification is the process God uses to make us more like Jesus).

> O Lord, you have searched me and known me!
> You know when I sit down and when I rise up;
>   you discern my thoughts from afar.
> You search out my path and my lying down
>   and are acquainted with all my ways.
> Even before a word is on my tongue,
>   behold, O Lord, you know it altogether.
> You hem me in, behind and before,
>   and lay your hand upon me.
> Such knowledge is too wonderful for me;
>   it is high; I cannot attain it.
> Where shall I go from your Spirit?
>   Or where shall I flee from your presence?
> If I ascend to heaven, you are there!
>   If I make my bed in Sheol, you are there!
> If I take the wings of the morning
>   and dwell in the uttermost parts of the sea,

even there your hand shall lead me,
   and your right hand shall hold me.
If I say, "Surely the darkness shall cover me,
   and the light about me be night,"
even the darkness is not dark to you;
   the night is bright as the day,
   for darkness is as light with you.
                        Psalm 139:1–12

The attributes of God are all over this psalm. I'll focus on two: God knows everything (he's omniscient) and he is everywhere (he's omnipresent). First, see what it says about God's omniscience. God knows *everything* that could ever be known. And not merely abstract things—like knowing the answer to all of the math problems you could ever dream up or how many angels can dance on the head of a pin—he knows your very thoughts (v. 2). Each and every one. He knows the words you speak before they're on your tongue (v. 4). He knows when you rise and when you sit (v. 2). Are you sitting down right now? God knows. And he knew it from eternity past. Not only does God know *your* sitting and rising, he knows it about every person who has ever and will ever live.

God knows all of it. His knowledge is comprehensive, exhaustive, and into the details. He has never missed a thing, and he maintains all of this knowledge effortlessly. Monitoring the entire world demands no energy for God. Incredible!

But there's more. Consider what it says about God's omnipresence.

According to the psalmist, God is everywhere. He's in heaven (v. 8), on the sea (v. 9), and no attempt to avoid him will succeed (vv. 7, 12).

You can hide things from your parents and your friends, but you can't hide a thing from the Lord. Nobody has ever "pulled a fast one" on God. You can use camouflage to hide from an animal or another person, but it doesn't work with God. You have zero privacy with God. Even if you put up the most frightening sign on your bedroom door, you're never really alone.

How would you react if you found out someone was constantly watching you? You'd probably flee, right?

Remember the sins that David committed in 2 Samuel 11? He committed adultery, and then arranged the death of the woman's husband. David knew his sin was no secret; he knew he couldn't hide. Nobody else might have known David's sin but God. David knew the truth of Psalm 139:7: "Where shall I go from your Spirit? Or where shall I flee from your presence?" David knew the answer to that question: nowhere. You can't go anywhere to escape the presence of God. Not heaven. Not Sheol. Not the uttermost parts of the sea. He's there.

When you grasp these truths, you will know that God is even in the deep recesses and corners of your mind. You are not alone. You could be America's most wanted fugitive, living in a hole where no one can find you, and you would still be living your life before an audience of one. God knows you and God is with you. He knows everything you *do* and everything you *think*. And he's everywhere. All the time.

When I was younger, I remember my mentor Tommy pulling me aside. I respected Tommy immensely, so when he said, "We're going to talk," he had my attention. (I could still take you to the exact spot where this conversation happened.) Tommy had noticed that I was talking rudely to some girls, and he knew it wasn't right. I didn't think he noticed my actions, but when I realized that he saw and heard and did not approve, there was nothing I could do. I admitted that I was in the wrong and I decided to change. I had a good kind of fear of Tommy because I knew him and respected him. And when

I found out that he knew about my behavior, it forced me to change immediately.

My sin was not a secret with Tommy around. And God knows infinitely more than Tommy. It's been said that "secret sin on earth is open scandal in heaven." God knows what you're doing.

God is not like your friends at school. He's not like your parents. This is God Almighty. When you grasp who God is—including his omniscience and omnipresence—you will have a high view of God, and you will fear him like you should.

You've Got to Know to Grow

If you want to grow into a godly man or woman, these verses of Psalm 139 can be instrumental to your growth. That's the whole point of having a high view of God, that you know him and then live your life in response. So if you grasp these verses and understand what they say about God, and if you lodge them into your heart and mind, that means that every time you choose to sin you will have to set aside what you know about God. The more you know about God, the more you will be rejecting each time you choose to sin.

This is why Jesus prayed, "Sanctify them in the truth; your word is truth."[4] God uses the truth of his Word to remove sin from our lives and to increase our reverent fear of him.

When I make the choice to sin, I have to ignore all that I know from Psalm 139. This psalm presents a gargantuan speed bump on the road to sin. Remember, God knows all things and is in all places.

If you've been tracking with what Psalm 139 says about God, you should want to respond like David did: "Such knowledge is too wonderful for me; it is high; I cannot attain it" (v. 6). Or, in the Dumas version of the Bible: "That. Blows. My. Mind."

I didn't understand this until I came face-to-face with Jesus Christ for the first time when I was a twenty-one-year-old PK (pagan's kid). Before that I thought there were no consequences to my actions. I could sin freely because nobody saw or knew, so it didn't matter. I was wrong. Dead wrong.

When you see our God as he really is, you will quickly become serious about him and his role in your life. The Creator of the universe—who knows all things and is in all places—is not to be trifled with.

Do you know what it means to be a creator? Have you ever made something with your hands? Think about it: If you use your hands to make something, like a birdhouse, or a cake, you set the rules for how it functions, what it looks like, right? That's how it is with God. He made us, he made the universe, and he gets to set the rules.

To Fear Is to Love

In order to fear God, you must have a high view of God. And to have a high view of God, you must know that he sets the rules. The next step is to *do what he says*. In other words, to fear God—your omniscient and omnipresent Creator—is to obey God. That's why Solomon said our whole duty is to "fear God and keep his commandments."[5] To fear God is to obey God, and to obey God is to love God.

The way you live your life will display what you believe about God. You cannot claim to fear and love God if you refuse to do what he says. You can't tell me that you love your mom and dad while you continually ignore their instructions. That's not how it works. The apostle John has some strong words for people who think this way: "Whoever says 'I know him' but does not keep his commandments is a liar, and the truth is not in him."[6]

If you have a high view of God, you will keep his commandments. If you have a low view of God, it will be obvious in the choices you make.

So get wise: Fear God and live like it.

2

Know the Bible and Pray Like Crazy

Every word of God proves true; he is a shield to those who take refuge in him.

Proverbs 30:5

If your aim was to run a marathon a year from now, you'd come up with a training plan to get ready for the 26.2-mile gauntlet. Otherwise, if you just jumped in and tried to run the race with no training, you'd be left with some serious damage to deal with. If you decided you wanted to be a doctor, you must know there are years of training ahead of you. Nobody wakes up with the ability to do surgery.

In 2014, I ran a race called Tough Mudder. I didn't do enough training leading up to the race, as I naïvely thought the twelve miles of mud and cold, with challenging military-style obstacles along the way, would be no problem. Needless to say, that assumption was wrong. I finished bruised, electrocuted, cold, and fatigued. I raise my orange headband (the finishing trophy) to all the crazy ones who've done it with far more training than I did.

The same thing goes with your spiritual growth. Nobody wakes up with godliness figured out. It won't happen on its own. You've got to train yourself for godliness.

This was Paul's message to his young protégé, Timothy. He told Timothy, "Train yourself for godliness; for while bodily training is of some value, godliness is of value in every way, as it holds promise for the present life and also for the life to come."[1]

Since God's Word is timeless, sufficient, complete, and always relevant, Paul's message applies to your life. Anyone who is in Christ should want to grow in godliness, and everyone in Christ has two vital tools by which to train themselves: the Bible and prayer.

I'm twenty-nine years into the Christian life, and the disciplines of Bible study and prayer are just as indispensable now as they've ever been.

Do you want to hear from God? I mean, really hear his voice? Then read your Bible. Those are his very words. God wrote one book, and we need to know that book. Do you want to speak with your Maker? Then pray. He really will listen. He really will answer.

It's possible to be around Bible study and around prayer regularly without actually being a young man or woman of the Word or of prayer. If you change your patterns in these categories, it will change your life. It's that important. I'm not trying to shackle anyone with a new law, but I want you to know how important these things are for your growth as a young person. All of the disciplines are important (fasting, fellowship, serving, evangelism), but these two—Bible study and prayer—are at the top of the list.[2]

Bible

Before I became a Christian, I never wanted to read. Part of why I entered the military was so I wouldn't need to study in college. When God saved me, he also gave me a real passion to read. And it wasn't just a passion to read the newspaper—it was to read his Word and books about the Bible. When I look back on my life, I can see that reading the Bible and reading about the Bible have caused the most spiritual growth in my life.

As a young person, you should desire to know God's Word. The Scriptures should be your treasure and your pleasure. Make it your priority. To know the Bible is to know God. Christians are to have the mind of Christ, and we do that by knowing his Word. How else will we learn to love what God loves and hate what God hates without knowing what he has said to us? It's impossible.

Satan will work tirelessly to distract you from prayer and Bible reading. Nothing messes with him more than to see God's people spending time in prayer and studying the Word.

I would like to see you grow more passionate about the Bible, and I will do that by sharing with you what Scripture means to me in my life. I'm going to give you a few attributes of Scripture and how these attributes function in my life. You'll notice I reference Psalm 119 a lot. That's because Psalm 119—the longest chapter in the Bible—is a poem dedicated to the Bible.

Scripture is my guide. Psalm 119:105 says, "Your word is a lamp to my feet and a light to my path." When life is dark and gloomy, I'm going to look to God's Word, and it will light the way forward.

Scripture is my treasure. Psalm 19 says God's words are of extreme value:

The law of the LORD is perfect,
    reviving the soul;
the testimony of the LORD is sure,
    making wise the simple;
the precepts of the LORD are right,
    rejoicing the heart;
the commandment of the LORD is pure,
    enlightening the eyes;
the fear of the LORD is clean,
    enduring forever;
the rules of the LORD are true,
    and righteous altogether.
More to be desired are they than gold,
    even much fine gold;
sweeter also than honey
    and drippings of the honeycomb.
Moreover, by them is your servant warned;
    in keeping them there is great reward.

vv. 7–11

Scripture is my protection. Psalm 119:11: "I have stored up your word in my heart that I might not sin against you." It's simple: Either sin will keep you from Scripture, or Scripture will keep you from sin.

Scripture is my authority. Scripture gets the final say in my life. Isaiah 66:2 says that God is near the one who trembles at his Word. We should want that to be us. Those are the kinds of people that God will use to do great things.

Scripture is my all. It is completely sufficient, lacking nothing. Second Timothy 3:16 is massive for this point. Scripture is God-breathed, profitable to make us qualified for every good work. I love Paul's words here. He says that Scripture is good for teaching, for reproof, for correction, and for training in righteousness. God's Word is sufficient for all of it.

Scripture is my revealer. Scripture exposes my pride and my sin. If I ever think too highly of myself, I just need to read my Bible. Sometimes I'm a phony, and the Word calls me out. There's nothing more sobering than the Scriptures. They wake me out of my slumber and delusion. The Word reveals and exposes our motives.

Scripture is my food. I can't live by bread alone, but by the words that come from God's mouth. God's people crave the Bible the way a baby craves milk.

These are just some of the attributes. There are many more we could name, but these are the ones that stick with me.

The point is this: The Bible is a nonnegotiable aid in your spiritual growth. The Word saves you and sanctifies you. You'll never outgrow the Bible, and it is essential to your spiritual formation. If you don't know the Bible, you're handicapping your sanctification.

Amazingly, what you'll find as you read the Bible throughout your life is that you won't get bored with it. There's always more to know. The Scriptures are written in a way that they can be easily understood, like a shallow puddle that you can splash around in. But they're also like an ocean that you can dive into without ever reaching the bottom. It will widen and deepen with each year of your life.

So read your Bible. This is the first and most critical discipline of your life as a young person. You show me a well-worn Bible, and I'll show you a strong Christian. And there's not just one way to do it. You can read your Bible at night, in the morning, whenever. It's less important *how* you do it, and more important *that* you do it. You've got to make time for it.

There aren't any tricks, just discipline. If you read three chapters of the New Testament every day, you'll get through it in three months. When I first became a Christian, my mentor told me to read three chapters of the Old Testament, three chapters of the New Testament, one psalm, and one chapter from Proverbs every day. I did that every day for years, and I have benefited immensely from that instruction. I was unfamiliar with the Bible, so devouring Scripture like that was pivotal to my formation as a person.

Prayer

Next to Bible reading, prayer is the most important part of your life. We need to learn to pray. Again, I'm not putting a law on you. God doesn't want you to be burdened with guilt. If you're in Christ, he loves you and will give you nothing but grace. One way to access that grace is through prayer. Prayer is an invitation to know God and see him answer.

A lot of Christians struggle to pray. Why is that? Why don't we pray? I would suggest three possible reasons, though there are more:

1. **Indifference**—we don't believe it matters or that it changes anything.
2. **Independence**—we think we can handle everything without God's help, as though we can muscle our way into the kingdom.
3. **Importance**—we don't think it's an important part of our life compared to everything else going on.

Can you relate to any of these struggles? I think most of us can.

Sometimes we feel like praying is a weak thing to do. Well, guess what? It is weak. But God loves to use weak people, because in our weakness, he shows himself to be powerful. And he loves to use a bunch of weak Christians who are willing to pray. So many important moments in church history were sparked by a group of people getting together and praying.

Does God answer every prayer? Yes. He'll respond with Yes, No, or Wait. He knows what's best for us, so even his No responses are as good for us as a Yes.

We too often think of prayer as a luxury, but it's a necessity. It's not an option. It's sinful *not* to pray. There aren't specific requirements as far as time goes; it's about doing it as naturally as you breathe. Pray big, bold, specific prayers. Pray fervently and frequently.[3]

One significant motivator for me is in knowing how much Jesus prayed. One example comes from Mark 1:35: "And rising very early in the morning, while it was still dark, he departed and went out to a desolate place, and there he prayed." Prayer was a central part of Jesus' life. He taught his disciples how to do it, he healed people by it, he was able to face the cross through prayer, and, incredibly, the last words he spoke on the cross were in prayer. That's Jesus Christ, the King of Glory. If he needed to pray, how much more should it be a part of *our* lives?

Prayer should be our first response to every situation, not the last. God should be the first person you run to for refuge. The devil would rather you do anything than pray. William Cowper, a great songwriter, said, "Satan trembles when he sees the weakest saint upon their knees." Let's make Satan tremble.

Just as with Bible reading, there are a lot of ways to pray. The Bible is full of different kinds of prayer: adoration, lament, thanksgiving, petition, confession, and more.

I like to use the acronym ACTS: Adoration, Confession, Thanksgiving, Supplication. It starts with worship, which naturally leads to confession. From there, you give God thanks for all he has done for you, and then you bring him your supplications (requests).

You can use the Psalms to fuel your prayers. The prayers of others provide a sure guide, like *The Valley of Vision: A Collection of Puritan Prayers* by Arthur G. Bennett. Get together regularly with some friends to pray.

This may not work for you, but this is how I do it: I have a box of 3 × 5 index cards with different categories of requests on them: things to pray for daily, weekly, and monthly. I take one card from each of those categories and pray for the things on it. So on any given day, I'm praying for something urgent like a friend with cancer; I'm praying for something consistent like my family, other pastors at my church, or my lost neighbors; and I'm praying for something a little less urgent, like a friend from seminary who I keep in touch with. That way, I don't get overwhelmed with all the things I can pray for, and I don't feel like I need to get everything in at once. God knows my needs.

Early in my Christian life, my mentor told me to pray for thirty minutes after reading my Bible. So I listened, and it changed my entire trajectory. Not long after that, I asked a friend to help me pray *better*. So he told me to come pray with him, and I just sat and listened to him pray. I learned how to pray by listening to him.

Discipline in the Disciplines

If you want to make Bible reading and prayer consistent disciplines in your life, develop routines. Pick a time, a place, a strategy, and a goal. I have a certain chair that I use, and my kids know what I'm doing when I'm sitting there. But it can be anywhere—sitting on your bed, at the kitchen table, wherever you feel comfortable—so that when you get there, it's natural for you to start reading and praying.

As someone with a military background, I understand the value of discipline. Discipline brings restrictions, but it also brings results. A routine might feel stale once in a while, like you're just fulfilling a duty, but your soul needs routine. As John Piper said in a sermon, prayer and Bible reading are duties:

> ". . . the way it's the duty of a scuba diver to put on his air tank before he goes underwater. It's a duty the way pilots listen to air traffic controllers. It's a duty the way soldiers in combat clean their rifles and load their guns. It's a duty the way hungry people eat food."[4]

Reading your Bible and praying is not about doing something just because it's a luxury. It's about survival.

You have access to God. Never forget that. You have access to his mind through his Word, and you have access to his throne through prayer. Those are two incredible privileges. It's up to you to take full advantage of this access. Make a habit of hearing from God in his Word, and communing with him in prayer. Then just watch him change your life as a result.

3

Love the Church

Whoever isolates himself seeks his own desire; he
breaks out against all sound judgment.

Proverbs 18:1

Everyone has a desire to belong. It's natural to want to be part
of something greater than ourselves. Whether it's belonging to
a team, a band, or a club at a school, regardless of the sort of
group, we all desire to belong to something.

There's one group, though, that wins the Most Important
award every time, and that's the church. How do we know it's
so important? It's the one and only institution that Jesus died
for.[1] He promised to build his church, and that the gates of hell
will not prevail against it.[2] The church is important to Jesus,
and it should be equally important to his people.

Why Should I Care?

I used to think the church was boring and irrelevant. Maybe you can relate. Well, guess what: I was wrong. I love the church because Jesus founded it, died for it, and loves it. And I certainly want to be on his side. I love the church because God made the church to be the custodian and caretaker of the truth. Paul called it "the church of the living God, a pillar and buttress of the truth."[3] Healthy, biblical churches are where the truth is taught, modeled, promoted, supported, and cherished, and I want to be on the side of the truth.

If you claim to be a disciple of Christ, then you should be a part of a local church. In the New Testament, there was no such thing as an independent or lone ranger Christian. The early church assumed that Christians would belong to a body of believers. Being a disciple and a church member are the same thing. Now, I'll let your parents and your pastors decide at what age you should become a member, but either way, a local church is the place to be and attend regularly.

But let me give you a warning: There are *people* at church. In fact, the people *are* the church. The building is not the church. The property is not the church. The people are the church. And whenever people are involved, things can get messy. Relationships are never simple. Conflicts flare. People struggle with jealousy, gossip, impurity, and on and on. But God is at work in messy people who know they're imperfect and who run to Jesus to be cleansed. Jesus died for a sinful world.

Someone said, "The church is not a hotel for saints, it is a hospital for sinners." Whoever said that was exactly right.

I'm a pastor, so I get to see these things on a regular basis. I wouldn't trade it for anything. If the church was worth Christ's life, then it's certainly worth mine. There will be times when it's discouraging and it looks like the world is winning, but Jesus promised to build his church. When Jesus makes a promise like that, you can bet your life on it.

One of my favorite pastors was a man named Charles Spurgeon. He preached in London in the late 1800s. In 1891, he preached a message, challenging his congregation to give themselves to the church:

> Give yourself to the Church. You that are members of the Church have not found it perfect and I hope that you feel almost glad that you have not. If I had never joined a Church till I had found one that was perfect, I would never have joined one at all! And the moment I did join it, if I had found one, I should have spoiled it, for it would not have been a perfect Church after I had become a member of it. Still, imperfect as it is, it is the dearest place on earth to us.

Further, he said,

> As I have already said, the Church is faulty, but that is no excuse for you not joining it if you are the Lord's. Nor need your own faults keep you back, for the Church is not an institution for perfect people, but a sanctuary for sinners saved by Grace, who, though they are saved, are still sinners and need all the help they can derive from the sympathy and guidance of their fellow Believers. The Church is the nursery for God's weak children where they are nourished and grow strong. It is the fold for Christ's sheep—the home for Christ's family.[4]

The church is faulty, but it is also the dearest place on earth. It's not perfect, but a refuge for sinners saved by grace. So let me give you a few tips on how to get the most out of your church experience:

1. Try to be a part of the *whole* church. Youth group is great. A middle school or high school small group is great. But try to connect with people older than you, as well. They have so much to offer.

2. Don't just be a pew potato, sitting there for the sermon and then leaving. Be fully engaged. Pursue truth. Pursue mentors and wisdom. Find out what your spiritual gifts are and put them to use. If you want to put your gifts to work, it will happen *primarily* in the context of the local church.

3. Make meaningful relationships. You can't grow in solitude. Proverbs 18:1 says, "Whoever isolates himself seeks his own desire; he breaks out against all sound judgment." We all desperately need the kind of community that only the church can provide.

4. Take your problems to church. What I've found is that people run away from the church when they're facing difficulty. But we should do the opposite. The church is not for perfect people who have everything figured out. It's for messy sinners who have turned to Jesus for forgiveness and eternal life. You can bring your problems to your church. Church leaders are there to help you.

Healthy, Not Perfect

Pastor Mark Dever says, "There is no such thing as a perfect church. . . . But that doesn't mean our churches can't be more healthy."[5]

Don't even bother trying to find a perfect church. Every church has problems, and having a few problems does not mean it's not healthy. Do you know if your church is a healthy one? You should try to gauge whether it is or not. Or, if your family doesn't go to church, but you want to find one for yourself, I would strongly encourage you to find a healthy church that you can be a part of and give yourself to.

So what kind of church should you look for? To answer that we've got to look at one key passage from the book of Acts. This book, written by Luke, tells the story of the church just getting started and growing rapidly after Jesus ascended to heaven. It's a thrilling read. This passage, from chapter 2, gives us a glimpse of what life was like in the early church:

> And they devoted themselves to the apostles' teaching and the fellowship, to the breaking of bread and the prayers. And awe came upon every soul, and many wonders and signs were being done through the apostles. And all who believed were together and had all things in common. And they were selling their possessions and belongings and distributing the proceeds to all, as any had need. And day by day, attending the temple together and breaking bread in their homes, they received their food with glad and generous hearts, praising God and having favor with all the people. And the Lord added to their number day by day those who were being saved.[6]
>
> Acts 2:42–47

Notice that these people were "devoted." They were all in, not just hanging around the fringes. Even though you might be young, you don't need to wait to get involved. You can be devoted right now.

So what were these early Christians devoted to? Answering that question can help us determine what a healthy church should look like.

1. They were devoted to the apostles' teaching. Did you know that we still have the apostles' teaching? It's called the New

Testament. These early Christians were devoted to the Bible because they had the biblical authors still alive. We, too, should look for a church that prizes the Bible. Jesus said that his disciples abide in his Word.[7] For a church to be healthy, it's got to love God's Word. How can you tell if your church loves the Bible? Next time you're at church, take a look to see how much time is devoted to the Bible. Are there Scripture readings in the service? Is the sermon the highlight of the service? And is the sermon about a Bible passage every Sunday? If so, then that's a good sign.

2. **They were devoted to one another.** They shared with each other and cared for each other. These early Christians all loved Jesus and held the same faith, and that allowed them to have real fellowship. They treated one another like family, rejoicing and weeping with one another. We all need a church that has this kind of community. Does your church love to stay after the service and talk, or does everyone leave immediately? Is your church willing to help other church members in need?

   Churches should offer the kind of community that can't be found anywhere else on the planet. I experienced this when I was a pastor in Los Angeles. L.A. is a big entertainment city, and everything is so impressive and slick. As a church, we couldn't even try to compete with that stuff. If we would've tried to put on better shows than Hollywood, we would've looked like total fools. But what we could offer was community and fellowship. Hollywood does not offer the kind of community the church offers.

3. **They were devoted to worship.** If community is about our horizontal relationships with one another, then worship is our vertical relationship with God. The early church,

it says, was devoted to "the breaking of bread and the prayers." The "breaking of bread" was the Lord's Supper. The Lord's Supper is a beautiful opportunity to remember what Jesus gave in his body and blood. And they were devoted to prayer. We pray because we are so needy, and God loves to hear our prayers. We are utterly dependent on God, and we wouldn't want it any other way. God doesn't need our prayers, but we do. Christian people are praying people.

4. **They were devoted to the gospel.** Everything in the description in Acts 2 shows that these people believed the gospel and were committed to it. The gospel message changes everything. Why else do you think these people would spend so much time listening to the apostles, praying, and in community with each other? Because the gospel completely changed their lives. The same thing happened to me on June 22, 1986. That's a day I will never forget, because that's when I trusted Christ, and my life has never been the same. I've been part of a local church ever since.

The power of the gospel was on full display in the book of Acts in how they loved one another, how they worshiped, how they lived their lives, and how they cared for the people around them.

We should long to be in an environment like that, where people are totally committed to loving God and loving their neighbors. You're never too young to start investing in your church.

I wish I'd have been a believer younger in life, so I could have taken advantage of all the things you can. I missed out on all the camps, the church groups, the Sunday school classes. But since I became a Christian, I've been a part of the church, and I haven't left.

I don't want you to leave, either. There's too much to gain from belonging to something so big, so important, and so glorious. Jump in with both feet!

Part Two

You +
Others

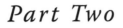

4

Submit to Authority

My son, do not forget my teaching, but let your heart keep my commandments, for length of days and years of life and peace they will add to you.

Proverbs 3:1–2

On December 26, 1984, I stepped off a bus and realized I was not as smart as I thought. That day was my first day of boot camp with the US Navy. It was still dark when I arrived, but I could see enough to know I was in a heap of trouble. See, I went into the military because I wanted to get away from my parents. I didn't like having them tell me what to do. Well, guess what happens when you go to boot camp? They told us when to sleep, when to eat, how long to eat, how to dress, where to stand, how to make our bed, how to shine our shoes, and everything else. This may surprise you, but they didn't use soft voices and kind words when they told us to do those things. Here I was, running away from authority structures, only to find myself in the most structured environment on the planet. Genius.

And yet, I am eternally grateful for that decision. The military completely reoriented my life. Even though I wasn't a Christian yet, I had enough sense to realize things were going to go really badly for me if I didn't submit to authority at boot camp. There were two options: Submit to authority or fail miserably. I didn't want to fail, so I shut my mouth, fell in line, and did as I was told.

What's Our Problem?

I don't know what kind of home you live in or grew up in. Maybe your parents are very structured and strict, and resisting their authority isn't an option. Perhaps you live in a free-range home, where you have a little too much freedom, and you end up dabbling in trouble because of it. But I don't need to know what kind of family life you have to know that you probably don't always enjoy submitting to authority. How do I know that? Because if you're reading this book, you're most likely an ordinary human being. And if you're a human being, you're a sinner, and sinners naturally chafe against authority.

Why don't we like to submit? It's pride and arrogance, mainly. We think we know all the answers. We believe our life would be better if we were in charge. Those are dangerous thoughts. Just ask Adam and Eve. That's precisely why Paul told the Romans that nobody should "think of himself more highly than he ought to think."[1]

We're all prideful and think we're better than we really are, but there are a couple of reasons why this is a problem for young people. It used to be that the way to gain wisdom and counsel was either to read a book or talk to someone older and wiser. Now, who are the first two people you talk to? Google,

Wikipedia? Are those your first two counselors? For some young people, older people have lost value when it comes to advice or wisdom. Trust me, I use the Internet, too, but it's important to know the value of older, more seasoned people. Textbook knowledge and human wisdom are not the same thing. Asking others for help is a good way to gain humility.

Submission is not something you outgrow when you get older. Everyone is under authority. Every person who has ever taken a breath submits to someone. We have laws that we submit to, teachers who make the rules in the classroom, coaches who decide what we do in practice, bosses who tell us how to work, and parents who set the guidelines at home. Even the Lord Jesus submitted to the Father's authority, doing only his Father's will.[2] It's amazing, isn't it? Jesus is not only a model for leadership, but for submission. We need both of those examples.

Why is submitting to authority such a big deal? Because submission and authority are woven into the fabric of the world God made. As God's people, Christians are called to submit to God and to his Word. If you're not willing to submit to a parent, a boss, or a teacher, then why do you think it will be easy for you to submit to God? Submission is critical to flourishing as a young person and as a Christian. The earlier you learn it, the better life will flow. Solomon said, "Length of days and years of life and peace they will add to you."[3]

The Bible calls us to submit to a number of authorities, but they all flow out of our primary submission to God.

Submission to God's Authority

God made the world, he made you, and he's in charge. The good life begins when you start listening to him more than to yourself. There's no higher authority than God, so submit to him while you still can.

One of the most important Bible passages for this comes from Proverbs 1. The first nine chapters of Proverbs are in the form of instruction from a father to a son. You can tell that the father is deeply concerned for his son. He's concerned that his son submit to the right authority.

In Proverbs 1:20–33, Solomon describes a unique scene with the beautiful and winsome Lady Wisdom standing at the intersection of the busiest city street, crying out for people to listen to her. She calls for people to submit to her ways, which are God's ways. But people keep walking by, not paying attention, thinking they don't need to listen. They reject her help and blow off her counsel. Here's the scene:

> Wisdom cries aloud in the street,
>   in the markets she raises her voice;
> at the head of the noisy streets she cries out;
>   at the entrance of the city gates she speaks:
> "How long, O simple ones, will you love being simple?
> How long will scoffers delight in their scoffing
>   and fools hate knowledge?
> If you turn at my reproof,
> behold, I will pour out my spirit to you;
>   I will make my words known to you.
> Because I have called and you refused to listen,
>   have stretched out my hand and no one has heeded,
> because you have ignored all my counsel
>   and would have none of my reproof,
> I also will laugh at your calamity;
>   I will mock when terror strikes you,

when terror strikes you like a storm
　　and your calamity comes like a whirlwind,
　　when distress and anguish come upon you.
Then they will call upon me, but I will not answer;
　　they will seek me diligently but will not find me.
Because they hated knowledge
　　and did not choose the fear of the LORD,
would have none of my counsel
　　and despised all my reproof,
therefore they shall eat the fruit of their way,
　　and have their fill of their own devices.
For the simple are killed by their turning away,
　　and the complacency of fools destroys them;
but whoever listens to me will dwell secure
　　and will be at ease, without dread of disaster."

Proverbs 1:20–33

Notice how concerned Lady Wisdom is for the passersby. She's holding out her hands, and at times attempting to grasp these people, offering them wisdom and life. These people hate knowledge, and they don't know the terrible things that await them. When she cries out, "How long?" you can feel her desperation. Because these people who won't submit to God's ways now may not get another chance. There will come a day when they will seek wisdom: "They will seek me diligently but will not find me," she says. Why? "Because they hated knowledge and did not choose the fear of the LORD." Simply put, they did not submit to the Lord.

Don't let that be true of you. If you're the kind of person who delays to following instruction, it will come back to bite you. If you procrastinate in submission and obedience, you will regret it, big time. When wisdom calls, and when God calls, you must submit.

Submission to Earthly Authorities

In addition to submitting to God, the Bible tells us other areas of life where submission is crucial. These areas are all part of your submission to God.

1. Submission to Parents

I'll bet this will sound familiar to you: "Children, obey your parents in the Lord, for this is right. 'Honor your father and mother' (this is the first commandment with a promise), 'that it may go well with you and that you may live long in the land.'"[4]

God was not careless in giving you your parents. They make mistakes (trust me, I am a parent), but the chances are good that they love you and want what's best for you. And when they tell you to make your bed or take out the trash, it's a good idea to listen. They know that patterns of submission are established in the little things in life, so that when the big ones come you are well practiced in the art of submission.

2. Submission to Government

The government exists to protect and maintain order in society, and to punish evildoers. It's there for our good. We should pray for our authorities.[5] We want to live peaceable lives in this age, so we should give thanks for our government. Jesus submitted to civil authorities—even telling us to pay our taxes!—and so should his people.

In Romans 13, Paul says, "Let every person be subject to the governing authorities. For there is no authority except from God, and those that exist have been instituted by God." God has put authorities in place, and if we disobey those authorities, we disobey God.

While in the military, there were many occasions that I had to salute an officer whose character and leadership I did not find particularly helpful. However, I learned early on in life to submit to authority even if that submission comes with gritted teeth. God honors those who honor others even when they disagree. You will come to find out that agreeing with government isn't always easy, but that doesn't alter God's call to submit to governing authorities.

3. Submission to Church Leaders

Your pastor and youth pastor are not perfect. Far from it. But God has required that Christians "Obey your leaders and submit to them, for they are keeping watch over your souls, as those who will have to give an account."[6] Your spiritual leaders are placed in your life for your spiritual progress and protection. To throw off their authority would be like pushing Lady Wisdom down to the dusty streets of ancient Israel.

Preparing to Lead

Are you sick of all this talk about submission? Let me give you one encouragement. One day, you will be in charge somewhere. Maybe you'll have children, or have employees working for you. Maybe it'll come sooner than you think, and you'll lead a Bible study in youth group or you'll be student council president. It'll happen someday. And here's what you should remember now: To be a good leader, you've got to know how to follow first. If you want others to submit to your leadership, you've got to learn how to submit to the authorities in your life.

Back in the 1990s (I told you I was old!), I learned this definition: Obedience is doing exactly what God says, when God says, with the right heart attitude (from Life Action Ministries). All three of those must be there to be truly submitting to authority. You have to be willing to submit promptly, and with a good attitude. Even if there's external submission (doing the right thing at the right time), you still might not be right internally (a wrong heart). All three conditions matter.

The earlier you learn this, the better you'll be able to lead later in life. For now, you've likely got more opportunities to submit to authority than to be an authority. So remember that God has placed structure in your life, and it is for your good. Wearing a seat belt in the car might feel restrictive, but it's there to protect you and maybe one day save your life. That's how submission works. Our submission trains us for godly living, and prepares us to lead in the future.

5

Serve Others

Whoever brings blessing will be enriched, and one
who waters will himself be watered.

Proverbs 11:25

The world applauds unhindered ambition. People who will do
anything to get what they want often get what they want in a
fallen world. It seems the only ones who get to enjoy this life's
perks are the people who "Look out for #1." If I am a "Dan-
oholic," that is perfectly acceptable and rewarded in our world,
because our world cheers for those who make themselves great.

The problem is, even though the world may applaud this,
God will not. Selfish ambition is idolatry and self-worship.
Idolatry comes from pride, and pride is that old and nasty sin
that caused trouble back in the garden of Eden. Pride removes
God from the center and places us at the center of our universe.
The pursuit of worldly greatness and renown is simply prideful
ambition, and God doesn't approve of it.

It's good to have goals, and to be ambitious to accomplish them. The difficulty comes in harnessing our ambition to use it for good and godly goals. There's a reason John Adams said, "Ambition is one of the more ungovernable passions of the human heart." We want to use our motivation and energy to serve other people. Jesus wants all his disciples to grasp that true greatness is defined not by who has the most money, the biggest house, the most power, or the greatest fame. Instead, greatness is defined by how much you serve.

The Diagnosis

If we're honest, we all want to be considered "great" people, and we would like people to recognize everything we do. If we're *really* honest, we even tell ourselves how great we are, and that we deserve more credit than we receive. This belief that we're truly great people is more common than ever, especially among younger people. David Brooks writes in his book *The Road to Character*, "In 1950, the Gallup Organization asked high school seniors if they considered themselves to be a very important person. At that point, 12 percent said yes. The same question was asked in 2005, and this time it wasn't 12 percent who considered themselves very important, it was 80 percent."[1] Self-importance and service don't work well together.

Some people are more honest than the rest of us in this regard. For example, the professional boxer Muhammad Ali exclaimed, "I want everyone to bear witness, I am the greatest! I'm the greatest thing that ever lived!"[2] Most of us (I hope) aren't saying those kinds of things.[3]

Even Jesus' twelve disciples spoke of greatness. Luke tells us about a certain conversation in Luke 22:24: "A dispute also arose among them, as to which of them was to be regarded as the greatest."

Did you catch that? Jesus' own disciples were debating about who was the greatest. That is not a good conversation to be a part of. But these guys were particularly dull to their context. This is a clinic in how to have an ill-timed and inappropriate discussion. A dispute about who's the greatest is never good, but it's even more pathetic when you consider that Jesus had just washed their feet (John 13), revealed that one of them would betray him (Luke 22:21–23), and was about to alter the course of history forever by going to the cross. But these guys were distracted by their own self-centered ambition.

Jesus responds to his disciples by teaching them. That's why he's the Lord and I'm not; I would've gone ballistic had I heard them. But not Jesus.

The Redefinition

After he overheard his disciples having their petty dispute, Jesus completely blew their minds by describing to them the path to true greatness:

> And he said to them, "The kings of the Gentiles exercise lordship over them, and those in authority over them are called benefactors. But not so with you. Rather, let the greatest among you become as the youngest, and the leader as one who serves. For who is the greater, one who reclines at table or one who serves? Is it not the one who reclines at table? But I am among you as the one who serves."
>
> Luke 22:25–27

This is a total redefinition of *greatness*. A game changer. Greatness is service. In God's world, the way up the ladder is the way down. This is a divine paradox. If we try to be great, then we will only grow small. Greatness isn't about entitlement or privilege, it's about service. It's about giving yourself away until it hurts.

The world has one view of greatness. The pursuit of power, money, fame, and possessions is expected and celebrated. If you can gather the most money, the most authority, and the most stuff, you win. Just think about the people our culture worships: wealthy celebrities. These are the "great" people. But Jesus says, "not so with you." It's completely different for God's people.

In God's world, the greatest people are those who serve the most.

Much Like the Great Physician

Let me give you an example of true greatness. Dr. Kent Brantly became well-known in 2014 because he was in the country of Liberia helping patients suffering from Ebola. There was a massive outbreak of the deadly virus in that part of Africa, and he wanted to help. He eventually contracted the virus himself, forcing him to come back to the U.S. to receive treatment. Dr. Brantly is clearly a servant, willing to serve those around him, even if it puts him at risk. And it doesn't stop there. He was serving with another medical missionary who contracted Ebola, and they only had enough medicine for one of them. Dr. Brantly insisted that it go to the other doctor. This man was willing to sacrifice his life for his patients and those around him. That's heroic leadership.

We could use a lot more Dr. Brantlys in the world. Not only doctors, but those willing to place themselves at risk for the sake of others. Servants.

Dr. Brantly recently spoke at the graduation ceremony at his alma mater, and he told them how he views his role as a doctor: "When everyone else is running away in fear, we stay to help, to offer healing and hope."[4] That's greatness: being willing to serve others, even when nobody else is.

A Gut Punch From Paul

The Bible has a lot to say about this kind of greatness. One great passage comes from Paul's letter to the Philippians.

Paul was concerned for his friends in Philippi. He knew selfish ambition and conceit (self-centeredness) is anti-Jesus. That's not how Jesus lived, and it's not how he would have his people live. Instead, he calls us to die to ourselves:

> Do nothing from selfish ambition or conceit, but in humility count others more significant than yourselves. Let each of you look not only to his own interests, but also to the interests of others.
>
> Philippians 2:3–4

Notice that Paul instructs us to "count others more significant than yourselves," and to "look not only to [your] own interests, but also to the interests of others." Biblically great people don't want to draw attention to themselves, but want to lay down their own lives for other people. You should be willing to serve other people because you should really believe they're more significant than you.

Take a Test

Here's a test (don't worry, this is not calculus) for whether you embrace this Christian definition of greatness: When someone doesn't give you the attention you think you deserve, how do you respond? To put it another way, if someone treats you like a servant, how do you respond? Do you feel offended and ripped off? If so, then you may be in pursuit of the wrong kind of greatness.

Another way to test yourself is to pay attention to the way you think about other people. If you're at the center of your universe, you probably have a low view of other people. If you have a biblical view of yourself, you will think highly of others. And when you think of others as more significant than yourself, you will be a serious servant of the King.

There's a catch to all of this. It's like a surprise plot twist at the end of a story. When God calls us to give ourselves away and serve others, he is not calling us to a life of misery. Just the opposite. The way of service and humility is the way of joy and satisfaction.

Worldly math: Pursuing my dreams and ambitions = temporary happiness

Godly math: Pursuing the good of others = lasting joy

I'll bet you've experienced that before. It feels good to do something for another person, doesn't it? The life of true greatness makes a habit of doing good things for other people, and not wanting any credit for it.

Our Supreme Example

One last thing to motivate you: When you pursue this kind of greatness, you are simply pursuing Christlikeness. This is how Jesus lived. He did everything for the sake of others. He told his disciples, "The Son of Man came not to be served but to serve, and to give his life as a ransom for many."[5] If Jesus—the one person who deserves to be served—was willing to serve others, who are we to do otherwise?

You might think, "This all sounds great, but I have no idea how I should do this." If that's you, try using this list as a way to get your imagination going for how you can serve your family, your church, your classmates, and everyone around you.

How to Be Great

1. Pray for other people. There's no better way to serve other people than to ask God to bless and help them.

2. Do chores around the house without being asked, and don't tell anyone you did it. This will freak out your parents. Take out the trash. Clean your room. Mow the lawn. Wash some dishes. Write a kind letter to your mom or dad.

3. Look for ways to do similar tasks at church.

4. Talk to the elderly people at your church. They love talking to young men and women like you.

5. Help a classmate with their homework.

6. Be friends with students who get bullied or mistreated.

7. Hold the door open for others.

8. Go with your family or your youth group to serve food at a homeless shelter.

9. Look for examples in your life. Who are the people who do all sorts of work for other people but don't get much credit? Those people are heroes. Imitate them.

10. Study Jesus, the prime example. How much of a servant was he? He left the glory of heaven and "humbled himself

by becoming obedient to the point of death, even death on a cross."[6]

There are all sorts of ways to serve other people. Life will bring you more joy when you remove yourself from the center. True greatness is found in the pursuit of God's glory and the good of other people. And you're never too young to be great.

6

Seek Mentors

Iron sharpens iron, and one man sharpens another.

Proverbs 27:17

In World War II, the Japanese military captured a vast number of POWs (prisoners of war). Having POWs is an important part of warfare because of the information those soldiers might know. The Japanese knew that their American prisoners had valuable information that could help their cause. So they used all sorts of tactics to break the resolve of those soldiers and get them to cough up any military secrets they knew. A lot of these tactics were physically brutal. But one of the more effective techniques was isolation. They realized that removal of all human contact would eventually break down a soldier's resolve.

In all circumstances, whether it's in warfare or the mundane routine of life, too much isolation will damage your soul. As a Christian, specifically, it's impossible to grow by yourself.

And as a young person, you need to have people older and wiser than you who will push you along in your growth as a Christian.

Too many Christians, especially young ones, try to figure things out all alone. They try to learn the Christian life by trial and error, and they end up with mostly error.

It's Always Been This Way

God did not design us to be lone rangers, but to walk with others and learn from them. If you don't think you need the advice and counsel of other people, then you need a little help. Just look at some of the Bible's instructions about this:

> Iron sharpens iron, and one man sharpens another.
>
> Proverbs 27:17

How do you sharpen a knife? By scraping it along a piece of steel. How do you sharpen your character? By living in close contact with other mature disciples of Christ.

> Whoever isolates himself seeks his own desire; he breaks out against all sound judgment.
>
> Proverbs 18:1

Isolation, according to the Bible, is just a bad idea.

> Then the LORD God said, "It is not good that the man should be alone."
>
> Genesis 2:18

It wasn't good for Adam, and it's not good for any of us for long periods of time.

Older women . . . are to teach what is good, and so train the
young women.

> Titus 2:3–4

The apostle Paul expected younger women to need help. The
same is true for young women today.

Urge the younger men to be self-controlled.

> Titus 2:6

Just like the young women needed to be trained, so do young
men. An older man can show you the way.

I urge you, then, be imitators of me.

> 1 Corinthians 4:16

Be imitators of me, as I am of Christ.

> 1 Corinthians 11:1

Join in imitating me, and keep your eyes on those who walk
according to the example you have in us.

> Philippians 3:17

Paul told Christians to imitate his way of life. We all need
people like Paul, whom we can look to as godly examples, who
are older, wiser, and further down the trail.

You get the point. God does not intend for us to learn godly
living on our own. Have you ever learned a language? If so, you'll
know that one of the best ways to learn another language is
to spend time with people who are fluent in it. If you want to
learn Spanish, talking with fluent Spanish speakers will greatly
aid your progress. So it is with Christianity. If you're a young

Christian, spending time with those more "fluent" than you will be a boon to your growth.

I know this because it's the story of my own life.

My Mentor

Besides my parents, my mentor Tommy, whom I've already mentioned, stands out above all others as the greatest influence in my own life. Much of who I am today (the good parts, at least), I owe to this man's life, example, and ministry. His life served as the most eloquent sermon I've ever heard. He was God's gift and means to assist me in personal growth. My life is evidence of his ministry, much like what Paul said to the Corinthians:

> You yourselves are our letter of recommendation, written on our hearts, to be known and read by all. And you show that you are a letter from Christ delivered by us, written not with ink but with the Spirit of the living God, not on tablets of stone but on tablets of human hearts.[1]

Paul didn't need a letter of recommendation to validate his ministry. The Corinthian believers were his letter of recommendation, the proof of his God-given ministry.

My own life is like a letter of recommendation for Tommy, who mentored me so intentionally and faithfully.

As I've said, I became a Christian at age twenty-one. Prior to that, I wanted nothing to do with Christianity. After I became a Christian, it took awhile for me to grasp what this "discipleship" thing was all about. For six months I just lived on cruise control, hardly reading my Bible, and not sure what to do. I did know that cruise control was not what Jesus meant when he said, "If anyone would come after me, let him deny himself and take up his cross daily and follow me."[2] Coasting is not cross-bearing.

God gave me a desire for spiritual growth. So I started to look around to see who was growing and progressing in their faith, and one guy stood out among the rest. His name was Tommy. He was one of the pastors at my church. I would sometimes observe him from a distance and think, *I want to be just like that guy*.

At this point, my Christian walk was more like a crawl. If I was ever going to run, I needed to run with those who did it well. If I just hung around people who were spiritually lazy, that's what I'd become, too. Tommy was running.

So I went to Tommy and said, "I need help." I had no idea how good of a decision I was making at the time. Besides deciding to follow Jesus, and deciding to marry my wife, this was the best and most important decision I've ever made.

Tommy taught me so much. Here are just a few things:

- **Cost.** He taught me and showed me that following Jesus comes at a cost. It means taking time to read the Bible and pray. It means using time, money, and resources to serve and bless other people.

- **Loving confrontation.** Sometimes his investment in me came with a sting. Tommy cared enough about me to correct me when I needed it.

- **Character.** Consistency mattered, and I saw it in Tommy's life. He told me how much is lost when I compromise my integrity, and he taught me how to deal with my sin because I saw how he dealt with his.

- **Challenge.** He gave me my first opportunity to preach, even though I was completely unprepared. He opened doors for me, let me stumble and fall, and let me learn.

- **Multiply.** After a few years, he told me it was time to take what I had learned and start mentoring other people. He pushed me out of the nest and told me to fly.

Those years with Tommy were some of the most fun and formative of my entire life. I long for you to find a relationship like that.

Where to Start

At this point, maybe you're excited about finding a mentor. I hope you are! By having a mentor, you're following in the path that Christians have walked since the first century. Even Titus and Timothy—guys who were pastors and had Bible books named for them—had Paul as a mentor. By the way, I'm sure you have great parents, and you should obey them in everything, but it's good to have a mentor outside of your family. An outside influence can be really helpful.

So how do you find your Paul? Good question. One thing to keep in mind is that chemistry is important. You can't just have a mentor assigned to you, because the quality of the relationship is important. Ask God to bring someone into your life who could be a mentor (there are no perfect mentors, so be realistic). After you pray, diligently look around and see if there is someone worth imitating. After you identify someone, take the initiative. If you don't know this person, introduce yourself and ask if you could meet. And of course, you can ask your parents for help finding a mentor. They might have a better idea than you do about who would be a good mentor (hard to believe, I know).

There's a myth about mentoring that says the best mentors are the most successful and prominent people. If that were true, few people would have good mentors, because the group of extremely successful people is quite small.

The best mentors are not spectacular. They're solid. They may not stand out in a crowd, but they will definitely stand out in heaven. That's true for Tommy.

I like to use a couple of acronyms to describe the kind of mentor/mentee relationship that will be good for your growth. When looking for a possible mentor, you can use the acronym THIN to identify four key things in a mentor:

- Time. Mentorship takes a commitment of time. Find someone who has the ability and willingness to invest time in you. Maybe it'll be a weekly meeting at the same time, or something more fluid.
- Holiness. Find someone whom other people respect and consult. Identify an older man or woman who lives a godly life and whom other people look to for advice.
- Imitation. Look for someone imitable.
- Need. This person has what you need. You know your weaknesses, and you want someone who knows how to address them.

When you find a mentor, you've got to hold up your end of the bargain. We used the acronym THIN for mentors, so for mentees we're using FAT (not original with me, but helpful). This is what you've got to be in your relationship with a mentor:

- Faithful. Be dependable. Show up on time, and be disciplined.
- Available. If you really want to be mentored, you'll be willing to make time and sacrifices when necessary.
- Teachable. Be humble enough to receive instruction, and be willing to change.

Multiply

There's always an expectation with mentoring, that once your mentor has invested in you all he or she can, you are to turn around and find someone you can mentor. It's about multiplication. As a young man or young woman, you must find someone older and wiser than you who can help you become a fully devoted disciple of Christ. And after some time—maybe a few years—you may find someone younger whom you can help become a more faithful disciple of Christ. Then, after some time, your protégé can mentor someone else, and so on. Multiply yourself.

When we let older and wiser people truly know us, they can help us. As Americans, we value privacy. We have fences around our yards, we tend to keep our front doors and bedroom doors shut, and we don't want anyone reading our text messages or emails. In other words, we want people to stay out of our business. But that is not the way to become more like Jesus.

We need to invite people *into* our lives, not keep them out. Iron doesn't get sharper by itself, and you won't either.

7

Choose Friends Wisely

Whoever walks with the wise becomes wise, but the companion of fools will suffer harm.

Proverbs 13:20

Sir Ernest Shackleton was an intense explorer. In the early 1900s, this British man led a number of expeditions to Antarctica. You know, the place where the temperature likes to hover around *negative* 70 degrees? On these expeditions, Shackleton endured poor health, shipwreck, hunger, and living on sheets of ice for months at a time. It was brutal. So brutal that he eventually died on one of the trips.

What kind of people do you think Shackleton wanted around him on these expeditions? If you had to go on a trip to Antarctica, who would you take with you? You could bring people who are a tad lazy, easily distracted, and undisciplined, who might be a lot of fun to be around, but who ultimately wouldn't help you reach your destination. Or you could bring people who are trustworthy, work hard, are humble, and would leave it all on the ice for you. Even if they were not as fun as the first group, you would trust them to journey with you, no matter how cold and nasty it got.

You would probably choose the second group. I would too.

We don't always get to handpick the people we work with—our teammates, classmates, or neighbors. But you have more control over who your friends are than you think. If you know what kind of people you'd want with you on an adventure to the Arctic, then you have a good idea of the kind of people you want with you as you adventure through life.

The Mirror of Friendship

"Bad company corrupts good morals." Have you heard that before, or something like it? Maybe your parents or your youth pastor have said something like, "You become like the company you keep." I hope this isn't disappointing, but your parents and youth pastor are spot-on.

They're right because the idea that our friends influence us comes right out of the Bible: The apostle Paul said, "Bad company corrupts good morals."[1] A thousand years earlier, King Solomon said, "Whoever walks with the wise becomes wise, but the companion of fools will suffer harm."[2]

Both Paul and Solomon make the same point: Choose your friends wisely.

This is no small matter. When you choose your friends, you choose a destiny. Your friends can determine whether you make it to Antarctica or not. This is why your parents care who your friends are. Your friends are like the food you eat. If you eat junk food all of the time, it'll start to show after a while. If you put yourself around bad influences, it'll start to show in your life.

If we spend a lot of time with bad company, then we'll become the bad company.

We need to find authentic friends who will be there when the weather is fair *and* when it's foul. We need a Proverbs kind of friend, the kind who "loves at all times," and who is "born for adversity."[3] Even more important, we need to *be* that kind of friend!

Spiritual Friends and Allies

I think a better word for the kind of people we want in our lives is *ally*—someone to journey and battle with through thick and thin, who will get dirty and walk through the valley of the shadow of death with you.[4]

Everyone needs spiritual allies and gospel friends. This isn't a modern invention. This is ancient wisdom, going back to Genesis 2:18, when God said, "It is not good that the man should be alone." You put that together with Proverbs 18:1, which says, "Whoever isolates himself seeks his own desire; he breaks out against all sound judgment," and you see that gospel partners come right from the mind of God.

How do we find a spiritual ally, and how do we become a spiritual ally or gospel friend? We want to choose the right people to be around, and we want to be the right kind of people. So what does it look like? What are the traits of these kinds of friends?

Timothy and Epaphroditus

A good place to find some guidance is in the life of the apostle Paul. In Philippians 2, Paul tells us about a couple of his closest friends, allies with him in ministry. Paul wrote this letter from prison, and he desperately wanted to visit the Philippian church, but prison made that impossible. So he sends them two trustworthy friends: Timothy and Epaphroditus.

Paul describes these two guys, and gives us some defining traits to look for in spiritual allies.

1. They're more concerned about others. Paul knew that young Timothy was a true ally in the faith. When he tells the Philippians that he's going to send Timothy to them, he says, "For I have no one like him, who will be genuinely concerned for your welfare."[5] Timothy is *genuinely concerned* for their welfare.

Paul knew a lot of people, but he has "no one like" Timothy! Timothy is a trustworthy friend to Paul and to the Philippians because he is concerned for the sake of others.

What are you most concerned about? When your friends or family have a problem, do you think about it and pray about it? When something good happens to your friends or family, are you happy for them? Take a look at the things you pray about most. Those are the things you are *genuinely concerned* about. For Timothy, it was other people. That's what he cared most about. Sounds a lot like Jesus, who laid down his life for his friends.

2. They put themselves last. In verse 21 of Philippians 2, Paul says this about the people who *are not* like Timothy: "For they all seek their own interests, not those of Jesus Christ." Ouch.

Earlier, Paul told the Philippians, "Do nothing from selfish ambition or conceit, but in humility count others more significant than yourselves. Let each of you look not only to his own interests, but also to the interests of others."[6] Paul knew people who sought their own interests. They cared most about themselves. Those are the people you can't surround yourself with. They will run when things get messy because they've got their own interests to pursue. They won't go with you all the way to Antarctica because they'll turn around when it gets too cold. But Timothy was teamed up with Paul, which was not an easy task. He wouldn't have done that if he were concerned with his own interests.

Who's first in your life? Would you forsake a friend just to pursue a goal? Or do you put yourself last?

3. They put it all on the line. There's another friend that Paul wanted to send to the Philippians: Epaphroditus. This guy didn't mess around. Paul described him as a "worker" and a "soldier." But not only that. Epaphroditus was serving Paul, and became so sick he nearly died.

Epaphroditus was distressed about his illness, but not for the reasons you'd expect. Epaphroditus was distressed because he didn't want the Philippians to worry about him. He wasn't distressed by his own condition, but how it affected others. He didn't mind that his work as a soldier and minister ran him ragged. He was willing to give it all.

Philippians 2:30 says that he "nearly died for the work of Christ." This guy was a stud. That's the kind of friend you can do battle with.

It's Up to You

You determine those who influence you. Find a Timothy or Epaphroditus. Attach yourself to people going where you want to go in life. Do you see people who are better students than you?

People who know their Bible better, or who are more mature in the faith? Then get to know those people. Spend time with them. As iron sharpens iron, let those people sharpen you.

Your friends are a mirror of your character, so be sure you like what you see.

Part Three

You +
Yourself

8

Take More Risks

Trust in the LORD with all your heart, and do not
lean on your own understanding.

Proverbs 3:5

A few years ago, I was on my way to Italy to teach the Bible.
I was with my friends Eric and John, and we stumbled upon
an advertisement to ski Mont Blanc. This would be a once-in-
a-lifetime opportunity, so we decided to go for it. We ponied
up the Euros and prepared to go the next day. After meeting
our guide (you couldn't ski without one due to the dangers),
paying for helicopter insurance (this was the only way off the
mountain if something went bad), and putting on mountain-
climbing harnesses, we made our way to the launch.

I could tell this was no ordinary adventure. The risk level
had reached an all-time high for me. I spent five years jumping
out of helicopters in the navy, in the pitch black of night and
in heavy seas, so I'm no novice when it comes to thrill seeking,
but this was a bit gnawing to the pit in my stomach. Backing

out was not an option, however, so away we went. I can recall numerous occasions on that multi-hour ride down the slope thinking, *I am a goner!* When we completed the run and finished our day, we were all pumped with adrenaline and thankful to be alive. I was thankful I took that risk.

Playing It Safe

Sadly, there have been other occasions when I didn't take the risk—whether it was not having a hard conversation with a friend, not boldly speaking up for the gospel with co-workers and neighbors, or something as simple as not trying some mystery food on a mission trip to Ukraine.

Those are moments when I was living by sight and not by faith. Risk-taking doesn't have to involve risking life and limb; it can be as simple as stepping outside your comfort zone, attempting new things, and giving yourself away.

We naturally want to avoid any risk. That's not altogether bad, of course. Your parents probably have insurance on the cars and house and other things to cover the risks involved of loss or damages. That's smart. The problem comes when we're not willing to do good, hard things because it might make us uncomfortable. We like our comfort, and our flesh is risk averse. No challenges, please. Not only does our flesh want to avoid risk, but the devil would love to sterilize any attempt at going *all-out* in this life. The flesh and the devil will pose numerous questions at the crossroads of risk-taking: *Why now? What are you thinking? Can one person really make a difference?*

We shouldn't take risks just so we can say we did it, or so we can pound our chests in pride, or to draw attention to ourselves. It is quite the opposite. We take risks for the sake of others.

Run Into the Building

On the ten-year anniversary of the terrorist attacks of September 11, 2001, I saw a story on TV about one fireman who was on the scene when the attack happened in New York. When everyone was leaving the burning building, he was going back in. He went up the stairs and kept climbing because he wanted to get to the impact area, where the most injured people would be. In this story, multiple people recalled seeing this one firefighter going up the stairs when everyone else was going down the stairs to get away from trouble. That's a beautiful picture of taking a risk for the sake of others.

Life will confront you with a million opportunities to "run into a burning building." If you live with your eyes open, you'll see one situation after another where something needs to be done, where someone could use some help, or where something needs to be said. Risk-takers will capitalize on those opportunities to help others address the problem. We want to pursue that kind of risk-taking.

Taking these kinds of risks call out the best in us. They require us to reject comfort and pursue something greater.

In his book *Risky Gospel*, Owen Strachan says, "It's not the *absence* of any challenge that will invigorate your life and mine; it's the *presence* of the right one."[1] That's what we're after.

Jesus didn't give his life so that we would sit on our backsides and play it safe. Jesus died so that we would get after it, trust him, double down, and take more risks. Jesus is asking us to live by faith and not by fear.

There was a Christian woman who was instrumental in the story of my conversion, and when I became a believer, she told me the first thing I needed to do was get a new Bible. I protested that idea. For one thing, I didn't like to read. But I also didn't want to be mocked in the military for carrying a big leather book around. I finally succumbed to the pressure, and got the smallest Bible I could find. The next thing she told me was to go out evangelizing with her that night. You can imagine how I reacted. I was completely out of my comfort zone. I had zero Bible knowledge. I had been a Christian for about twenty-four hours. And here she was asking me to come with her to share the gospel with total strangers.

She was taking a risk on me. That idea could have totally backfired. But what happened is that her bold example helped ignite in me a desire to see people embrace Christ. It would have been easier for her to go out evangelizing by herself, or take someone who actually knew what to say. But she took a risk by taking me.

A Gospel Bucket List

There's a choice before you. You can passively embrace comfort and play defense all your life, or you can pick up your game and play offense. One of the best ways is to develop a gospel bucket list. Set goals for risks you want to take, challenges you want to pursue.

There are all sorts of categories of life where you could take risks. Everyone's list will be different. For example, take a short-term mission trip to a remote place. Learn another language and use it to talk to someone about Jesus. Spend time caring for the homeless, helpless, and hurting. Read a minimum of twelve great books a year. "Adopt a child" by supporting a child in need overseas. Attend college internationally. Write a book. Discover a cure for malaria. Plan a fundraiser for missions. Build literacy cultures so that people will have access to the

Scriptures. The list is as long as your imagination. One thing is for sure: We are all called to take more risks.

You won't regret taking chances to benefit other people, but you will regret spending your life watching from the sidelines.

About a century ago, President Teddy Roosevelt gave a speech entitled "Citizenship in a Republic." His message is aimed right at us:

> It is not the critic who counts, not the man who points out how the strong man stumbles, or where the doer of deeds could have done them better. *The credit belongs to the man who is actually in the arena*, whose face is marred by dust and sweat and blood, who strives valiantly, who errs, who comes up short again and again, because there is no effort without error and shortcoming; but one who does actually strive to do the deeds, who knows great enthusiasm, the great devotion, who spends himself in a worthy cause; who at the best knows in the end the triumph of high achievement, and who at the worst, if he fails, at least fails while daring greatly, so that his place shall never be with those cold and timid souls who neither know victory nor defeat.

You can be that kind of young person. The person who's in the arena, who will fail and commit error, but who's willing to take the risk. Who will strive to do the deeds. Get in the arena and strive valiantly.

You don't want to get older and think, *Well, I got pretty good at video games,* or *I watched a lot of TV.* Those things aren't on your gospel bucket list. You're built to do greater things than that. William Carey, the father of modern missions and an ultimate risk-taker, famously said, "Expect great things from God; attempt great things for God." That would be a great motto by which to live. Now put this book down and make a plan to take more risks.

9

Work Hard

The soul of the sluggard craves and gets nothing,
while the soul of the diligent is richly supplied.

Proverbs 13:4

There are a lot of life skills that are better caught than taught. Do you know what an apprentice is? An apprentice is someone who learns by watching. An apprentice works for someone and imitates what they do. The best way to learn how to do carpentry is to watch someone do it so you can witness their expertise and ask questions along the way. It works in all fields. Musicians listen to other, better musicians. Athletes watch other athletes to learn how to improve their skills.

The Bible teaches this kind of learning. We benefit from good examples. But the Bible actually tells us—especially those who are lazy—to become apprentices of a surprising teacher. In order to learn how to work hard and be diligent, the book of Proverbs tells us to learn the craft from one of the smallest creatures in the world: the ant.

> Go to the ant, O sluggard;
>> consider her ways, and be wise.
> Without having any chief,
>> officer, or ruler,
> she prepares her bread in summer
>> and gathers her food in harvest.
> How long will you lie there, O sluggard?
>> When will you arise from your sleep?
> A little sleep, a little slumber,
>> a little folding of the hands to rest,
> and poverty will come upon you like a robber,
>> and want like an armed man.
>>> Proverbs 6:6–11

The tiny ant offers big instruction. These ants live with intentionality, gathering their food during the summer so they have enough food for winter. Did you know ants can carry more than fifty times their body weight? Imagine doing that. If you weigh 100 pounds, this is the equivalent of carrying around 5,000 pounds! These ants are tough as nails. They know how it feels to work hard.

But we don't go to the ant to learn how to lift weights. There are other things that set them apart as good teachers. Here are three lessons we all need to learn from the ant.

1. **Ants are self-starters.** They take the initiative to work, even "without any chief, officer, or ruler." The ant knows when it's time to get after it; they don't need an ant boss barking instructions to get things done.

When I joined the navy, it was clear that my superiors thought the only way to get us to do anything was to yell at us. And they were right! But ants don't need anything like that. They just take the initiative.

2. **Ants have foresight.** They predict and plan, preparing food in summer, gathering food in harvest. You've got to make plans thoughtfully and intentionally to get things done. If you've got work to do, set out a plan for how to do it, and then follow the plan. As someone aptly said, you've got to "plan your work, then work your plan." Do you have a book you need to read for school? Make a plan for how many pages you need to read each day and then execute your plan. Do you have chores to complete at home? Plan a time to do them. If you don't have a plan to get things done, you probably won't do them. To quote an African proverb, "How do you eat an elephant? One bite at a time."

3. **Ants are industrious.** They use their resources and reject laziness. They're not like the sluggard who lies there sleeping with his hands folded. No, the ant takes advantage of the time by working. The ant knows he's got to make the best use of the time, because it passes quickly.[1] And he knows poverty will strike if he doesn't work.

Taking Dominion

It's important for the ant and for you to have something to do. Idleness is no friend, especially when you're young. Having too much time on your hands will lead to your doing things you shouldn't do, going places you shouldn't go, and looking at things you shouldn't look at. Hard work is a gift from God to keep you from being distracted by worthless things. It's your friend, training you for a productive life.

This might surprise you, but hard work is not about the *kind* of work you're doing. You can do hard, manual labor and still be lazy. Hard work is about taking dominion.

When God created Adam, he put him in the garden of Eden and gave him a job: Take dominion over the garden. That was Adam's job, to take dominion over the garden by protecting it, growing it, and bringing order to it. This is *before* sin entered the world. Work was something God gave to humans before the fall. It wasn't until after Adam and Eve ate the forbidden fruit that God put a curse into work, when he told Adam, "By the sweat of your face you shall eat bread."[2] Work is a good thing from God, not a part of the curse.

Where do you need to take more dominion? Your bedroom? Your car? Your dorm room? If you constantly have a messy bedroom, you're not exercising dominion. You've got to clean it, organize it, and be in control of it. You have to learn to manage your life. What about your schoolwork? Are you always behind, doing things at the last minute, and forgetting what you need to do? Get organized and take dominion!

This is important, because young people are always tempted to be lazy. I was lazy. When I think back to my years in school, I know I could have gotten better grades, but I was a lazy bum. One semester, my parents offered me $20 for every A I earned. Guess who got straight A's that semester?

The danger is that the way you live as a young person will make an impact on the way you live as an adult. When my son Aidan was ten years old, I was at the dinner table with him as he stared down a bowl of broccoli. I was sympathetic; who likes broccoli, anyway? But I knew this was a moment for instruction. I looked at Aidan, then looked at the bowl, and said, "What do leaders do?" He replied, "Hard things." This may seem mundane, but that nasty bowl of broccoli provided an opportunity for a ten-year-old to demonstrate dominion and do the hard thing. He still remembers that moment. Don't think you can just wake up one day and start working hard after being a sluggard for fifteen years. You've got to develop patterns of hard work. Habits are formed early in life, so start making good habits now.

It's also important because hard work glorifies God.[3] And *every* kind of work glorifies God. It's not just Christian activities that glorify God. A pastor and a farmer can honor God just the same. You can glorify God by making your bed and doing your homework just like you can glorify God by going to church or reading your Bible. Glorifying God, as the *Westminster Catechism* states, is the chief end of man. The apostle Paul states that whether you eat or drink or whatever you do, do it all for the glory of God. There is both glory and dignity in doing hard work. We are built for doing hard things.

Start and Finish

One hundred percent of people struggle with procrastination. We wait until the last minute to get something started. What I try to do to fight against procrastination is make a daily list of what I need to get done, and I do the hard things first. I know if I can get those things done, then I've got some good momentum, and I can get all kinds of things accomplished. But if I have those hard things always hanging over my head, waiting for me, it's going to be tough to do anything else.

Procrastination—not being able to start—is one side of the problem. The other side is not being able to finish. These are the people who are always starting things and always zealous for something new, but never finishing. An unfinished life is not worth living.

One year, my son was on a really bad baseball team. It's no fun playing on a team that loses all the time. So one day he came up to me and said, "Dad, I think I'm done." To which I replied, "No, you're not. You're going to play every single game." Quitting wasn't an option for him, and it shouldn't be an option for you. If you let yourself quit in things like baseball, then you're going to want to quit when you face more difficult things. And trust me: You will face more difficult things. It's vital that you finish what you start.

Negative Examples

The ant provides us with a good, positive example. But we can learn things from bad examples too, right? Well, Proverbs gives us such an example, called a *sluggard*. Here are some lessons from the sluggard:

1. He Won't Finish What He Starts.

The sluggard buries his hand in the dish and will not even bring it back to his mouth.

Proverbs 19:24

Lesson: The sluggard never finishes anything. He is willing to put his hand into something but is too lazy to finish the job. Make yourself a finisher. Be the kind of person whom others can count on to see something through.

2. He Won't Listen.

The sluggard is wiser in his own eyes than seven men who can answer sensibly.

Proverbs 26:16

Lesson: Don't think so highly of yourself that you don't seek advice. It's easy to be arrogant when you're lazy—if you never do anything, you won't learn your own limits. Work hard, and ask questions along the way.

3. He Makes Excuses.

The sluggard says, "There is a lion outside! I shall be killed in the streets."

Proverbs 22:13

Lesson: The sluggard always has an excuse not to do something. He is unwilling to face obstacles; he just runs away from them. Don't make excuses, just make something happen.

4. He Wants Things But Won't Work.

The soul of the sluggard craves and gets nothing, while the soul of the diligent is richly supplied.

Proverbs 13:4

The desire of the sluggard kills him, for his hands refuse to labor. All day long he craves and craves, but the righteous gives and does not hold back.

Proverbs 21:25–26

Lesson: The sluggard wants something, but a hard worker is willing to plan and work for it. Stop worrying about wanting the next big thing, and start working hard to earn it.

5. He Doesn't Plan Ahead.

The sluggard does not plow in the autumn; he will seek at harvest and have nothing.

Proverbs 20:4

Lesson: The sluggard won't make plans. He has no foresight, and lives only for the moment. If you can't think of the future and how to plan for it, you're in for a hard lesson.

Get Working

I hope the takeaway is crystal clear: You don't want to be a sluggard. The Bible has nothing good to say about lazy people. If you want to excel as a young person, and please God with your life, then start working hard now. Focus. Make plans. Start things and finish them.

Working hard will help those around you. You will be a good example to others. You'll likely do well in school and at home. And you will bring glory to God. You don't have to be a body builder, and you don't need to imitate the world's richest people. Just look to the ant, and be wise.

10

Make Character King

The righteousness of the blameless keeps his way
straight, but the wicked falls by his own wickedness.

Proverbs 11:5

Nobody respects someone who talks a good game but doesn't
live a good game. People who loudly proclaim their own greatness are already obnoxious, but especially when they can't back
it up. The smallest package in the world is a person all wrapped
up in themselves.

The world is in desperate need of young men and young
women who are committed to living a good game. We need
young people who aren't concerned about promoting themselves, but who let their life do the talking. Those students
whose private lives and public lives are in sync, keep their word
and value character.

There are some good examples of this kind of living. One
example is Wayne Gretzky. For those of you who don't know,

he's a former professional hockey player, known simply as "The Great One." If you open an NHL record book, you'll find his name everywhere. He was charged (falsely) for being involved in a gambling scandal, but his former teammates and coaches quickly came to his defense. They recalled how carefully he carried himself, how he never gambled (even where it was legal), didn't stay out late with teammates, and never went into a bar underage. He knew how important it was to maintain a clean reputation.

Building and maintaining your character like that is asking for challenge. The battlefield of character is littered with fallen soldiers. We are all called to live exemplary lives, and if you don't have character or integrity, nothing else matters.

God values things differently than the world does. He measures our success and our value, using a very different scale than the world does. In some parts of our culture, people are valued by how beautiful they are. In the professional world, people are deemed successful by the skills they possess and how much money they earn with those skills.

In God's world, we are only as successful as our character. If we portray ourselves a certain way but act like a different person behind closed doors, then we're just faking it, and nobody likes a hypocrite.

That's why Robert Murray M'Cheyne said, "It is not great talents God blesses so much as great likeness to Jesus."

Your Life

One of my favorite verses in the New Testament is 1 Timothy 4:16. Paul tells Timothy, "Keep a close watch on yourself and on the teaching. Persist in this, for by so doing you will save both yourself and your hearers."

Did you catch those first six words? "Keep a close watch on yourself." He's not calling us to stand in front of a mirror for hours on end. He's calling us to watch ourselves with vigilance in order to preserve and grow our character.

To watch yourself well, you've got to play offense and never let your guard down. You've got to look for weak spots in your life and address them immediately. The secret service might let someone jump over the fence to the White House, but you can't let someone breach the threshold of your integrity.

The devil prowls like a lion, and he can find his way through weak protection. The stakes are too high to take it lightly; heaven and hell hang in the balance. Having a well-ordered life is critical to everything you will do in the future. The Bible calls you to die to yourself, but it also calls you to watch yourself. God is more concerned with what we *are* than what we *do*. Character is king.

Your Doctrine

The second thing Paul tells Timothy to keep a watch on is the teaching (doctrine). Doctrine is simply another way to refer to the things you believe about God. It's important that you keep watch on what you believe, even if you're not going into ministry like Timothy was. There are all sorts of false teachings out there, and people will present them like they're the truth. If you watch your doctrine, you'll know how to distinguish between truth and lies. The convictions you develop by knowing doctrine are the bedrock for building solid character.

As a teenager, you've got to watch both your life *and* your doctrine. Life without doctrine is dangerous. Doctrine without life is hollow. They're equally important.

True doctrine will give backbone to your character, so you'll be able to stand in any situation. In fact, doctrine is vital for your growth as a Christian because it teaches us how to live. The truth exists to set us free, so we've got to know it.

High Stakes

If you had to walk a tightrope that was five inches off the ground, you likely wouldn't be nervous. The consequences for a fall aren't that great. You would just step off the rope and try again. But what happens if you raise that tightrope to five stories above ground or over Niagara Falls? Different story. The graver consequences would warrant greater care.

When Paul urges Timothy to watch himself, he gives him two reasons that raise the stakes to extraordinary heights: "Keep a close watch on yourself and on the teaching. Persist in this, for by so doing you will save both yourself and your hearers."

Watch your life and doctrine, because you'll save yourself and your hearers. (*Note:* I know you probably don't have many "hearers" right now, so we'll focus on the first part.) It doesn't get any more serious than this. Eternity awaits. Your soul is at stake.

What does Paul mean? Does he mean that we can save ourselves, and that we can save others? I thought salvation was by grace alone through faith alone in Christ alone! Of course, that's true. Paul hasn't changed his mind since he wrote Ephesians 2:8–9.[1] Salvation is of the Lord.

Yet, incredibly, God uses people to get things done. He uses broken, messed-up people to change the world. He promises to complete the work he's begun in us,[2] and our commitment to character is one of the ways he'll do it.

A Portrait of Character

It's common for young people to be unsure of what they believe and how they should live. They're looking for direction, so they just follow everyone around them. The world doesn't need any more followers, it needs young men and women with the character to lead and stand up like Job.

Do you know the story of Job? He was an incredibly wealthy man, with all sorts of livestock. That was how wealth was gained, by having livestock and land. Job was rich and, more important, a godly man. He loved the Lord. The devil wanted to see just how much Job loved God, so God gave Satan permission to test Job. So one day, a messenger came to Job and told him some terrorists had attacked his oxen, his donkeys, and his servants. Another messenger came and said fire from heaven had destroyed the sheep and the servants. Another messenger said some other guys stole the camels and killed more of the servants. There went his whole livelihood and the ability to maintain employees. The last message was the worst: A tornado had destroyed the house of Job's oldest son during a family reunion, killing all of Job's children.

All this is in one day. It's a total onslaught. A nightmare.

Job's response to Satan's best efforts defines biblical character: He gets up, tears his robes, shaves his head in grief, falls to the ground, and *worships*. And when his own wife tells him to curse God, Job refuses, and says, "Blessed be the name of the Lord." That's strong and indomitable character.

We know that this response wasn't a fluke for Job. He spent his entire life building his character and doctrine so that when the crisis struck, he had the capacity to respond with integrity.[3]

Watch This

I want to pass on to you a few categories to use as you watch your life. I'll never forget the first time I heard someone describe these four areas. It literally caused me to pull my car over to the side of the road and take notes (this was probably illegal, but I was having my world rocked).

Before we get there, a word of caution for those who can take the admonition "watch yourself" too far, who become so introspective that they become paralyzed from ever taking a step forward or leading.

When you examine your life, don't look at things minute-by-minute, or even day-by-day. Rather, look for the direction your life is headed, month-by-month, or every six months. All day long we are up and down in terms of walking in the Spirit. You can't take your spiritual temperature anytime. Look for progress, not perfection. Paul actually told Timothy to ensure that "all may see your progress."[4]

Personal holiness is a lifelong process. You will never outgrow your need to grow. The Bible promotes grace-induced progressive sanctification (that's a five-dollar phrase).

Let me encourage you that you can lead a blameless life, not because of your own strength, but because of what Jesus has done in you and for you. Jesus wouldn't expect something of us that was impossible to do.

So many get frustrated and quit because they claim the expectations are too high. Blamelessness is not sinlessness. Only Jesus lived a sinless life on this planet. Blamelessness is knowing how to deal biblically with your sin when it rears its head in your life. No mere mortal is perfect, but among the imperfect there are the blameless, and they're the people who know how to deal with their sin.[5] More important, you know the One who ultimately dealt with your guilt and sin by dying on the cross.

These categories can help you plan your progress, because these are areas where young people especially, and all people generally, are prone to struggle:

1. **Slothfulness.** Idleness is no friend of integrity. Laziness will kill. Hard work is good for the soul.

2. **Silver.** Money's not bad. Loving it is. It can control you and become the primary way you think about your life. Remember what Jesus said: You can't serve both God and silver.

3. **Self.** Do not put *yourself* at the center of your life. Love God and love others.

4. **Sex.** Sexual immorality in all its forms will destroy (just read the next chapter and you'll see).

These are broad categories that entangle the majority of people, so use them to keep a closer watch on your life.

I want you to live with no regrets, with abandonment, and to experience the joy-filled Christian life. God is so brilliant and kind that when he tells us to live a certain way, he's laying out a path of life that will bring no regrets and all kinds of joy.

A young man or woman with strong character will stand out like a diamond in the dirt. A student with serious integrity is tragically rare. If you make character king in your life, people will notice, your life will be joyful, people will follow you, and God will use you in big ways.

11

Flee Sexual Immorality

For the commandment is a lamp and the teaching a light,
and the reproofs of discipline are the way of
life,
to preserve you from the evil woman,
from the smooth tongue of the adulteress.
Proverbs 6:23–24

Fight or flight. It's a choice you'll make over and over again.
Usually "fight" is the right answer. It's better to dig deep, fight,
and lose than to quit or run away from a challenge. It builds
strength of character.

But occasionally the best response is to flee. If you're in the
path of a tornado, it won't do much good to stand your ground
and throw punches. Run to the lowest spot possible.

The book of Proverbs, that ancient fount of wisdom, lets us listen in on a father advising his son to flee.[1] The advice is relevant for daughters too, of course.

In Proverbs 5, the father tells his son that he will one day face temptation. The temptation will be appealing and promising, but in reality it is nothing but bitter poison. This temptation will not lead to life and joy, but to death and despair.[2] This temptation is the ensnarement of sexual immorality.

Sexual immorality is a broad category. What does it include? It includes any sexual activity that takes place outside of marriage. Lust, pornography, premarital sex—a whole gamut of other issues. It's the promise of doing something that may feel right but will only bring serious trouble.

The father in Proverbs continues his instruction by telling his son what to do when he encounters this woman:[3] "Keep your way far from her, and do not go near the door of her house."[4] In other words: Flee! Get out of there!

If you're a young woman or a young man, and you're in a situation where you need to make a quick response against sexual temptation, just run away. Don't think. Just run.

I've been there before, and you can't sit there and think about it. Sin makes you stupid. If you sit and think about it, you'll come up with reasons why the sin isn't so bad. You've just got to run away. By God's grace, that's exactly what I did. I was caught in a moment where I suddenly had to make a decision: either give in to temptation or flee. And I fled. *Literally*. I actually ran away—and probably looked like an idiot—but I'm okay with looking like an idiot for a moment if it keeps me from making a mistake I'll regret forever.

As someone said, if you don't want the fruit of sin, then don't hang around sin's garden. Ditch the garden. The young person who eats this forbidden fruit will regret it. Trust me on this.

Furthermore, trust Solomon, who told his son that sexual sin will cause him to say, "How I hated discipline, and my heart despised reproof! I did not listen to the voice of my teachers or incline my ear to my instructors."[5] This kind of sin always brings regret.

If you're reading this book, you're receiving instruction. Do you go to church, youth group, or camp? Maybe all three? You've probably received instruction. If you have ever read your Bible, you have received instruction. But when you sin, you are forsaking all of it, and you're saying, "This fleeting sensation is more important to me than all I've learned." You're deciding to ignore all the warnings and teaching you've received about sin and about God's holiness. Sin makes you stupid.

Growing up in the home that I did, I was well-acquainted with sin. Certain forms of sin were allowed in our house, and some of that sin falls into the category of sexual immorality. Many young men and women struggle with these same problems.

It used to be different, because some forms of sexual immorality were harder to commit when I was young. But along came the Internet, and things have changed completely. Everything is accessible, and you can remain anonymous. It can be easy to believe these problems aren't a big deal, since everyone seems to do it. Well, it is a big deal. A huge deal.

But the Bible says there are ways to experience victory in this area. Are you stuck in one of these sins? There's a way out.

I can say that confidently because that's been the story of my own life. I have seen victory in the area of sexual immorality, so I can tell you truthfully that there's a path of purity for those who are willing to fight for it. It's not that I don't feel temptation anymore, but I have a strategy for how to fight against it. And that's what I want to share with you. I'm not as smart as

Solomon, but here are my tips for how to stay away from the bitter poison of sexual sin.

1. Make No Provision for the Flesh

Paul tells us to "make no provision for the flesh, to gratify its desires."[6] A good way to "make no provision" is to avoid any dangerous situations. This is a way to play offense, so that you're not forced to react to temptation when it's already too late. Once your sinful flesh feels temptation, it's difficult to say no. Once you engage your flesh, it will take over until it is satisfied. And the promise of satisfaction is a lie. Your sinful flesh is never satisfied.

So if you enter a dating relationship, set clear boundaries for yourselves. Don't be alone with that person late at night; nothing good can happen. Spend a lot of time in groups of friends.

2. Accountability

Accountability can be a great tool in the fight for purity. Maybe you're asking, "What's accountability?" This usually involves your having one or a few friends that you meet with regularly to encourage one another to fight sin and pursue holiness. You ask about sin patterns, you confess sin, you pray for one another. Invite people to ask you how things are going in this area. It's good to bring our sin to the light; it has a better chance of dying there than in the dark.

Accountability is most useful when you combine it with other tools. It won't solve all of your problems on its own, and it's not foolproof. Accountability will only work if you fear God and truly hate sin. If you don't fear God, then you probably won't fear your accountability partner(s). If you don't care what God thinks of your sin, you won't care what your friends think.

3. Amputate

If you're struggling with sin, you've got to get aggressive. You've got to get serious about it. That's what Jesus wants you to do.

> You have heard that it was said, "You shall not commit adultery." But I say to you that everyone who looks at a woman with lustful intent has already committed adultery with her in his heart. If your right eye causes you to sin, tear it out and throw it away. For it is better that you lose one of your members than that your whole body be thrown into hell. And if your right hand causes you to sin, cut it off and throw it away. For it is better that you lose one of your members than that your whole body go into hell.
>
> Matthew 5:27–30

Jesus calls for radical action against sin. He doesn't mean you literally need to gouge out your eye or cut off your hand. But he does mean that sexual sin is serious, and you've got to take it seriously. If you're taking it seriously, you'll go to great lengths to cut this sin out.

Maybe it means you've got to shut down your Internet access for a while. Or get rid of your smartphone. Maybe it means you cut out PG-13 movies or a certain TV show. It would be better for you to get rid of those things for the sake of purity than to keep them and continue to sin.

4. Flee

As we noticed earlier, the Bible normally urges us to "fight" against sin. We're usually called to put on our armor of faith and fight for holiness—except when it comes to sexual sin. We're not called to *fight*; we're called to *flee*. In 1 Corinthians 6:18, Paul says, "Flee from sexual immorality." It's that simple.

The Proverbs use the language of fire. There is no playing with fire. If you try to play with fire, you will get burned. If you try to toy with sexual immorality, it will eat you alive. The thing with sexual sin is that it engages the body. The battle is not merely in the mind, it's in your actual flesh. You can't think your way out. You'll end up making a bad decision. The answer is simple: Stay away!

5. Grace

Remember, you don't need to sin. In 1 Corinthians 10:13, Paul says that for every temptation, there's a way out. You don't have to commit these sins. You don't need to look at pornography. You don't need to be a slave to lust. If you're a Christian, the Holy Spirit dwells within you, and he can give you the power you need to overcome sin.

Also remember that the Lord loves you. Jesus didn't die for perfect people; he died for sinners like us. And he wants you to be free from the power of sexual sin.

12

Embrace Correction

Faithful are the wounds of a friend.

Proverbs 27:6

Next time you're in a car, whether you're driving or riding along, pay attention to the poetry in motion around you. Notice how all of the cars on the road, headed to all sorts of destinations, in every direction, coordinate together. It's like a well-choreographed performance. If you look at a highway when you're up in a plane, the cars all move together like they're of one mind.

What's behind this organized movement? One big reason is simple: road signs and stop lights. Think about it: There are stop signs, speed limit signs, yield signs, street signs, exit signs, and signs telling you what highway is where. When drivers heed the instructions on those signs, there's order on the roads. If no one followed the instructions (and there are places around the world like that), there would be pure chaos. I met a student from Uganda once who was having trouble driving in the U.S.

because where he came from the rules were few, the road signs seldom, and the lanes nonexistent. Imagine how disorganized that would be!

The roads are not always safe in the U.S., of course. People drive too fast, ignore the signs, text while they drive, and crash their cars. But it's astounding what happens when everyone abides by the rules of the road. Because of that, most drivers actually appreciate the instruction on those signs because it improves the driving experience. This is an area where people understand that following instructions will make the drive smoother.

Welcome Warning

I saw this reality up close on a cold, snowy night a number of years ago, as I walked home from my friend's house. I saw a car approach a severe left turn, and the driver would need to navigate with caution. Sadly, there was no sign warning of the steep cliff on the other side. Well, that driver missed the turn. A mother, with an infant, drove straight off that cliff. Being alone, I raced to the hill, scurried down, and tried my best to help them. I could tell it was serious. They survived, fortunately, although they were seriously injured. All for the lack of a road sign. It was a warning of sorts.

Just imagine going down a road leading to the edge of a cliff, with no signs or warnings. Like that young mother, I'll bet you would want a sign on that road that said *Sharp Curve. Use Caution. Unprotected Drop-off Ahead*. You'd realize you were headed for something unusual, and you would be immensely grateful for the warning.

For you baseball fans, you've likely seen a base runner come flying around third base, only to stop suddenly because the third-base coach told him to stop. If he didn't stop, he'd probably get thrown out at home. If you've ever learned to play an instrument, your teacher probably told you things you could do better, or things you were doing wrong.

These kinds of corrections are immensely helpful, and we usually appreciate the correction. The Bible tells us that we should respond the same way to correction about how to live. That's the kind of correction we *all* need to hear.

Even the Wisest Man

Solomon was a smart man. He prayed to God to make him wise, and God answered generously. More often than not, Solomon had all the answers, and he was the one giving the instructions and correction. Yet being the wise man that he was, he knew "It is better for a man to hear the rebuke of the wise than to hear the song of fools."[1] Solomon understood that there is grace in admitting wrong and receiving correction.

Nobody likes to be told they're wrong, or that they need to change. It's humbling. It reminds us of our weaknesses. But what the Bible tells us is that it is good for us to receive correction. Left to ourselves, we'll make a ton of mistakes. If we're willing to admit when we're wrong, and to embrace correction, we will be putting ourselves in position for massive growth.

So we've got to embrace correction, and correction can come from many sources.

1. Friends

People say that a friend never stabs you in the back. That's true. A true friend will not stab you in the back, but he may hit you in the face. The principle here is simple: If you saw a friend standing in the path of a truck, would you love your friend enough to tackle him out of harm's way, or to at least yell, "Look out!" before the truck hit him? I sure hope so. A good friend is willing to inflict a little pain if it prevents a greater harm.

It might hurt a little for a friend to say, "Hey, I'm seeing this in your life, and it needs to change." But that's the kind of wound that will pay dividends in the future. King Solomon said it this way: "Faithful are the wounds of a friend."[2]

People boast about how open they are to change and correction, but seldom do they seek it. You can help this by making room (lots of room) for people to give you feedback. If you've got a mentor, ask him to show you areas in your life where you need help. Ask him or your parents for input. This is an instance where your parents are your friends. When they correct you, it's because they love you. If you've got a mature Christian friend who loves you, ask her where your blind spots are. When necessary, confess sin to people you've sinned against. If you're convinced you're not perfect, it'll be easier to handle when others know you're not perfect.

Personal correction from trusted friends is part of growing up in life.

2. Scripture

Another way we can receive correction is through God's Word. You might say these writers are our friends, wounding us from centuries ago! The Word of God is "living and active, sharper than any two-edged sword,"[3] and it can cut deeply. This will happen as you read your Bible regularly, when the Spirit convicts you, and you choose whether or not to embrace the correction.

Scripture will also intersect with your life through the preaching at your church on a weekly basis (I hope) for the rest of your life. If the preaching is biblical, it is going to confront you with ways you need to change. The Bible is aimed at transforming your life. But you must reject the temptation to become a professional sermon listener.

A professional sermon listener is someone who does a decent but incomplete job of listening to sermons. This person can take great notes, and maybe even understand what the preacher said and what the Bible passage means. But this person fails to *apply* the sermon and the passage to his or her life. God did not give us the Bible only to teach us and inform us, but to rebuke us, correct us, and transform us.

Jesus' half brother, James, wrote some important verses about this:

> But be doers of the word, and not hearers only, deceiving your-selves. For if anyone is a hearer of the word and not a doer, he is like a man who looks intently at his natural face in a mirror. For he looks at himself and goes away and at once forgets what he was like.
>
> James 1:22–24

A professional sermon listener is a "hearer" only. That's not enough. When a sermon or a Bible passage confronts us, we've got to obey and apply it. We've got to be "doers" of the Word.

If God's Word calls us to change but we aren't willing to embrace the correction, we may run out of chances to be truly changed. Let James hit you in the gut one more time: "Who-ever knows the right thing to do and fails to do it, for him it is sin."[4]

Don't just hear the Word, heed the Word.

3. God

There will be times when correction comes not from a friend, not from Scripture, but directly from God himself. The writer of Hebrews makes this point like a charging rhinoceros. In these beautiful verses, he compares the way that our earthly fathers discipline us in order to correct us to the way God does the same, as a loving Father:

> For [our earthly fathers] disciplined us for a short time as it seemed best to them, but [God] disciplines us for our good, that we may share his holiness. For the moment all discipline seems painful rather than pleasant, but later it yields the peaceful fruit of righteousness to those who have been trained by it.
>
> Hebrews 12:10–11

God's corrective discipline is painful, but it brings holiness, peace, and righteousness. We don't know when this will happen or what it will look like. But we do know why it happens: because God wants us to be holy, and he wants us to love him above all.

Sometimes it hurts to get stitches, or to get a shot, but in the long run it's for our good. The best way to purify metal is to put it through intense heat. The process may hurt, but the result will be glorious. The older I get, the more my appreciation grows for the many corrections I've received from various sources in my Christian walk.

Correction Is Kindness

Few things are more humbling than receiving correction and rebuke, and yet it's a sign of maturity. Correction is a hard gift from God, but a necessary one. The sooner you embrace it, the faster you will be able to make corrections and save yourself from costly errors. If you, as a future leader, refuse to receive correction, you're putting yourself above others, above Scripture, and above God. I hope that fact alone is enough to make you jittery. Correction isn't easy, but it's critical for our growth. Make a habit of seeking correction. Be relentless in this arena. Receive it, and embrace it. It may just be the Lord's kindness to you.

Part Four

You + the Gospel

13

Know the Gospel

> For our sake he made him to be sin who knew no sin,
> so that in him we might become the righteousness
> of God.
>
> 2 Corinthians 5:21

Time for a popquiz: Who was the eighteenth president of the United States? Did you know the answer right away? If I gave you ten seconds, you could search it pretty quickly. For those of you who don't want to do that, the answer is Ulysses S. Grant.

Next question: What's 2 + 2? I'll bet you didn't Google that question. You knew the answer. In fact, you hardly thought about it. The simple math is so fundamental that answering it took about as much energy as taking a breath.

Last question: What's your favorite food? The answer for that question isn't on the Internet, but you know the answer. In fact, you know this answer differently than you know what 2 + 2 is.

You don't just *know* what your favorite food is, you've tasted it. And every time you answer this question, you remember how good that food is. Your answer about your favorite food comes with personal experience behind it.

What would you say if I asked you, "What is the gospel?" Do you know the answer?

On one hand, this question is like the simple math equation because there's a right and a wrong way to answer it. 2 + 2 does not equal 5, and there are beliefs out there that are not the gospel. And just because someone knows how to answer the question "What is the gospel?" doesn't mean they know the gospel personally, the way you know your favorite food.

It's got to be both. You've got to have a solid answer (head) to the question, "What is the gospel?" But you've also got to know it deeply and personally (heart), the same way you *know* how your favorite food tastes.

As a young person, you're going to encounter different belief systems, worldviews, and people who don't like the gospel. So you've got to know it. You've got to know it with your *mind* and with your *heart*.

The Problem

Beginning in 1348, something called the Black Plague decimated the continent of Europe. It lasted just a few years but killed almost one-third of Europe's population, making it the most deadly pandemic in human history. You can see why it's sometimes known as Black Death. It took just a week for someone to contract the plague and die. One week. Oozing, black tumors would break out, followed by a series of awful symptoms. It was a brutal way to go.

At the time, nobody knew the cause, but they attributed it to the judgment of God. It was eventually learned that the plague came from fleas on rats that got to Europe on the Silk Road.[1] Unfortunately, knowing the cause did not eliminate the cost.

There's another plague you should know about. It's 100 percent fatal, causing both physical and eternal death: sin. Sin is a plague that can't be bound, blacker than anything fleas or rodents can carry.

The apostle Paul once called himself "the chief of sinners."[2] He knew this plague well, and it infected him deeply. But he knew that sin infects all people. "All have sinned and fall short of the glory of God,"[3] Paul wrote.

Whether you're the chief of sinners or relatively tame in your sin, you've fallen short. It doesn't matter how short you've fallen. If I tried to jump across the Grand Canyon—and broke the world record for long jump in the process—I would still fall to my death. Jumping three feet or thirty feet wouldn't matter. You would die either way. That's how it is with sin. Nobody gets a pass; we all fall short.

The Bible says we're sinners, and our lives show it too. We may not be as sinful as we could be, but we're still sinful through and through.

It all goes back to the beginning. Adam and Eve were created perfect and sinless, but Eve followed the snake, Adam followed Eve, and no one followed God.

Adam couldn't foresee the consequences of his actions, but they were weighty. When Adam sinned, he earned death for himself and all who would come after him.[4] He turned the world on its head, and we are all like him. We all look like our first father by our sinful nature and choices, sneaking around our own gardens, fleeing from God because our relationship with him is broken.

The Solution

So what do we do with this plague? How do we fix this problem and restore our relationship to God? The answer is the gospel. You've got to know how to answer that question. You've got to know the gospel, and all you need in order to grasp the gospel is one verse. That's it.

The New Testament was written in Greek, and this verse—2 Corinthians 5:21—is fifteen words long (in Greek). They're the fifteen most important words you'll ever read. Don't miss them. This verse says, "For our sake he made him to be sin who knew no sin, so that in him we might become the righteousness of God."

Martin Luther, the great Reformer of the church, called this "the great exchange." We receive what Jesus deserved, and he received what we deserve.

Our problem is that our actions have separated us from God, and we on our own can never get ourselves back to him. If it were going to happen, God would have to do it all. Thankfully, he did.

So what did God do, exactly?

He Became Sin

Our verse says, "For our sake he made him to be sin who knew no sin." He (God) made him (Jesus) to be sin. Wait. Jesus *became* sin? But it says that he knew no sin. How does that work?

What does it mean that Jesus knew no sin? It means Jesus was perfect. His character and moral fiber was impeccable. Sinful people can only be saved through a sinless Savior. That means that all of humanity is immediately disqualified from being the Savior. Except Jesus. He knew no sin. He knew what sin was, but never committed it. He was the spotless Lamb put forth as a sacrifice, the substitute for our sin. The Old Testament sacrifice system required a spotless lamb to serve as a picture of God's demand for a perfect sacrifice for humankind's sin.

If Jesus never sinned, how did he *become* sin on our behalf? He didn't become a sinner. He didn't die for his own sins. Rather, all of our sins, and all the sins of the world, were laid upon him. He was treated *as if* he were the worst of sinners.

Before we go on, I want to teach you a new word: *impute,* or *imputation.* If I set a building on fire, then tell people that you did it, I'm *imputing* guilt to you. If your neighbor accidentally knocks over your mailbox, but you think he did it on purpose, you are *imputing* a motive to him that wasn't really there.

When we're talking about Jesus and imputation, we're saying that God *imputed* our sin to Jesus, and he *imputed* Jesus' righteousness to us. God imputed our guilt onto his Son, so that Jesus was treated the way sin deserved to be treated. The wrath and penalty for sin was laid upon him.

He became our substitute. We deserve death and hell, but Jesus willingly stood in our place. That's how much he loves you.

When you work at your job, you earn a wage. When you get your paycheck, it's not a gift; it's what you've earned. The Bible says that the wages of sin is death. We sin, and we earn death. That's our paycheck. But God put forth Jesus to take our place, so he received what we deserve. He became sin *for us.* And we get eternal life.

All that we deserve—the entire penalty that we earn by our sin—was placed in Christ's account. And all that he earned by his perfect, sinless, righteous life is credited to the account of all who believe in him and his sacrifice for us. This is a pretty good deal, isn't it? This is the gift of all gifts.

John MacArthur hits the nail on the head: "God treated Jesus on the cross as if he had personally committed every sin ever committed by every person who would ever believe." Knowing this truth will change your life forever.

So That

Why did this happen? There's a purpose clause in this text:[5] "so that . . ." Paul tells us why God made Jesus to be sin: so that we might become the righteousness of God.

God did this so that sinners might become the righteousness of God. God *declared* us to be righteous. But that doesn't mean we automatically *become* righteous in our life. The reality is that you've still got sin to deal with. You've still got problems that you need to fight against. You've been declared innocent, free, and forgiven in Christ. Jesus has paid the penalty of your sin, and he will give you the power and the grace to fight against the sin that sticks around. He's given the Holy Spirit for this task, God himself, to dwell in you.

This is what sanctification is all about. As you know and believe the gospel, you will grow in the gospel, living more and more like Christ.

If you really know and believe the gospel, the progress in your life won't be immediate or magical, but it will be real.[6] Look at the direction of your life. When you leave high school, you should be more Christlike than you were when you started. When you finish college, you should be more mature in your faith and character than you were when you graduated high school. That's the gift of sanctification. That's becoming the righteousness of God.

So What?

Jesus became sin so that you can become righteous. Jesus endured the wrath of God for you. It should be very clear, then, that Jesus doesn't want to be a part of your life. He wants to be your entire life. When you take part in the great exchange, it's not a nice addition to your life. It's a total renewal.

In 1986, I was twenty-one years old and a proficient sinner. I never would have read a book like this. I grew up in a Christless, semireligious home, living my own life and full of myself. But God came looking for me. Let me assure you, I was not looking for him. I was happy in my rebellion. But God wouldn't leave me like that. He interrupted my life, and I learned that Jesus took my sin so that I could have his righteousness. I was stupid when I was twenty-one, but not so stupid that the Spirit of God couldn't open my eyes to see how good of a deal this is.

There's a good chance that some of you reading this book are exactly where I was when I was twenty-one. You haven't surrendered to the lordship of Jesus and let him reign in your life. You haven't turned away from your sin and trusted in Christ for forgiveness. You've got to deal with the plague of sin in your life, and there's only one way for that to happen: "He made him to be sin who knew no sin, so that in him we might become the righteousness of God." The great exchange. The sweet exchange. Jesus left the paradise of heaven for the ghetto of earth for people like you and me.

Know this gospel. Taste it. Believe it, and never let it go.

14

Speak, Defend, and Spread the Gospel

The fruit of the righteous is a tree of life, and whoever captures souls is wise.

Proverbs 11:30

Sometimes I hear Christians talk about how exciting it would be if someone famous in the music industry, or other public-exposure profession, would become a Christian. You can see why this might be exciting. These are incredibly successful people, and they carry a lot of influence. It would be great to see them use their influence for Christ (not to mention putting their trust in Jesus for their own sake). But we know, of course, that God also loves to use weak and insignificant people to do great things for the gospel.[1]

And those of us who are weak and insignificant could learn a thing or two from these successful people.

I contend that we need to be more enterprising with the gospel, thinking of creative ways to use our time, talents, and money to see the gospel advance. But before we get too creative, remember that the most important tool we have in sharing the gospel is our voice. We've got to open our mouths and tell other people what Jesus Christ has done for sinful people: He lived the perfect life, died the death that we deserve, rose from the dead on the third day, and brought salvation to all who will repent of their sins and trust in Christ for forgiveness. That is the good news, and that is what we must tell. We're not trying to grow our brand or get rich and famous. We're trying to spread the gospel as ambassadors for Christ.[2]

Don't Forget the Mission

It can be easy to grow lazy and forget the purpose that God has for us. One of the last things Jesus told his disciples was to take the gospel to the ends of the earth, and make disciples of all nations. There's a reason those verses in Matthew 28:18–20 are called the Great Commission. This is our mission, and it is a daunting task. But don't get lazy. Get fired up, and use your imagination to spread the gospel.

That's precisely what the parable of the ten minas can do for you. This story, from Luke 19, can help light a fire under your desire to share and spread the gospel. Stories like this are what have kept me motivated in gospel ministry for twenty-seven years. They make me want to be relentlessly engaged in speaking the gospel.

In this parable, Jesus tells a story. The story is of a wealthy, important man who was going to leave for a while. Before he left, he called ten of his servants and gave them some money, telling them to engage in business with that money.

This would be like someone giving you $300 and saying, "When I come back, I want you to have made that $300 into $3,000." How would you do that? Maybe set up a killer lemonade stand, or use the money to buy a lawn mower and start cutting grass for people in your neighborhood. In Jesus' story, the man wants his servants to invest, and to work hard so that the money he gave them brings in more money.

The Responses

There are two responses highlighted in the parable, and we can relate to each one. We're all represented by one of the responses. They are faithful obedience, or sad silence. Let's see how these servants did.

The first servant was a stud. He put faithful obedience on full display. He took the mina and increased it by 1,000 percent. That's impressive. Notice his humble response: "Your mina has made ten minas more" (v. 16). He doesn't say, "Look at what I did, and look how creatively I did it!" No, he doesn't take credit for anything, he simply reports what happened.

And the response he gets from the master should inspire us: "Well done, good servant!" (v. 17). Those words should be the aim of your life; to hear the Lord himself commend your faithful work.

Guess what he gets for a reward: more work! He's been faithful with what he was given, so now he's put in charge of ten cities. His hard work hasn't earned him a life of sleeping in, unlimited video games, and endless vacation—but more work. We should work to be ten-city people, like this servant.

Factoid: The reward for good, faithful work is always going to be more work. That's true in all of life. If you're a hard worker and a trustworthy young man or woman, people will look to you to get things done. And that's a good thing.

The second servant is faithful too. He took his mina and turned it into five more. Not as outlandishly impressive as the first servant, but still strong. His reward is much like the first servant's: He gets to manage five cities.

Both the first and second servants have been faithfully obedient. That's one way to respond to the task.

The third servant, however, has not been as productive as the first two. This guy has wasted his opportunity. He has nothing to show for his (lack of) effort. He was given one mina, and he still has it because he was too afraid to take any risks. He said, "Here is your mina, which I kept laid away in a handkerchief" (v. 20). In other words, he did not do what the nobleman told him to do. He refused to engage in business with the mina. There's a word for that: disobedience.

Then he blamed it on the master! "I was afraid of you, because you are a severe man," he told the nobleman (v. 21). He was too scared of the guy to do anything. This isn't the good kind of fear we talked about in chapter 1, the kind that brings wisdom and motivates obedience, but the kind that paralyzes people into inaction and sad silence.

That sad silence brings a harsh response from the nobleman. He called this third servant a "wicked servant." Not good. The nobleman then takes this servant's mina and gives it to the guy with ten minas.

Your Response

Well, here's the deal. In Jesus' story, the wealthy, important man represents Jesus, and the servants represent any who profess to believe in Christ. And the money he gives us—the minas—is the gospel. It's almost like the task he gives them: To "engage in business" is another way of saying, "Go, and make disciples."

If you're a Christian, then you're one of the servants. The nobleman gave his servants minas, then left. But the servants knew he was coming back. It's the same thing for us. Jesus came once, did his work, gave us the gospel message, told us to spread the news, and then left. But we know he's coming back.

What are we supposed to do with the gospel before Jesus returns? How do we respond with the instruction to "engage in business" with the gospel?

We respond by seeking to tell people the good news. That's how we multiply our mina. We have a mandate to speak and to spread the gospel of Christ.

If you're a Christian young man or woman, you already know the gospel. But you might need a spiritual shove toward your responsibility while you live on this earth. I mean, if the point of Jesus' life, death, and resurrection were only to get us saved, then he'd zap us to heaven as soon as we believed, right? That's not the point. Jesus leaves us here so that we can change the world by spreading the news of the gospel.

Don't be like the third servant. Don't be paralyzed into silence. If you truly believe that Jesus died for you and forgave all your sins so that you can have eternal life, but you never want to tell anyone about it, then something's wrong. The Lord does not want you to hide the gospel in a handkerchief. He wants you to engage, take risks, talk to your friends, and be bold with the gospel.

The difference between opening your mouth for the sake of others and staying silent in your comfort zone is the difference between "Well done, good servant" and being called a "wicked servant."

On Mission

We are called to live on mission. It isn't good enough to just go to youth group or small group every week, and church every Sunday, hear the gospel, and then stick it in your pocket as if it means nothing. We all naturally talk about the things that are most important to us. I'll bet your parents talk about you a lot. I'll bet you talk about your favorite musician or athlete or best friend a lot. What we spend time talking about reveals what's important to us, and what we love most.

So you should open your mouth and tell non-Christians about Jesus. That's engaging in gospel business. And who knows, maybe you'll be a young woman who turns one mina into ten, or a young man who turns his mina into five.

Life and Lips

Sometimes doing gospel business will take the form of defending the gospel. That's part of the New Testament expectation for spreading the gospel. When the occasion calls for it, we are to defend the gospel with both our life and our lips. Both are essential, neither can be muted.

The short letter of Jude was written in an attempt to "contend for the faith."[3] The need to stand up and contend for the faith is still urgent. You don't need to know every answer to every objection that someone has against Christianity. But you should always be "prepared to make a defense to anyone who asks you for a reason for the hope that is in you."[4] Equip yourself to know what to say when someone asks you why you believe what you believe. Tell them how the Bible makes sense of the world in a way that nothing else does, and that you believe Jesus rose from the dead, and nobody has proved otherwise.

If you want to contend for the faith, you've got to know *what* to say (lips), and *how* to say it (life). Paul tells us that when we deal with outsiders, we must let our "speech always be gracious, seasoned with salt, so that you may know how you ought to answer each person."[5]

If you truly identify as a Christian, you will meet people who disagree with you. These instructions from Paul are so important to remember in those situations. Our speech must be gracious, seasoned with salt, and our actions must be gracious too.

Don't let your conduct be like the prophet Jonah. God called him to preach to the people of Nineveh, and Jonah rebelled. He ran away, and the fugitive prophet found himself hiding out in the musty bottom of a cargo ship with a bunch of pagan sailors. When a catastrophic storm hit, these guys learned that Jonah knew the Lord, and the storm was his fault. Jonah articulated the things of God like an expert, but his life—his unwillingness to share the message of God's love—completely undermined his message.

Our actions can speak loudly, and they can help in our defense of the gospel. People might disagree with what you say, but don't let them disagree with how you carry yourself. The way you live will open doors for you to share the gospel.

The Challenge

I understand the difficulty involved. The task seems too huge, we are afraid of what others will think of us, or we're not sure how they'll respond. This task is too big for us, but not for the gospel. The gospel message is sufficient and powerful to save. Remember the Gerasene demoniac in Mark 5? That guy was possessed by demons. Living in a cemetery, he would cut himself, and was able to bust through any chains people put on him. If anyone was ever too far gone for the gospel, it was this guy. But that all changed the day he met Jesus.

And think of Saul, the chief of sinners, who terrorized Christians in the book of Acts, only to meet the Lord and have his life dramatically changed. He became Paul, the founder of untold churches and the most influential missionary in church history. The gospel is powerful enough to save guys like this. You might have friends and family you're scared to share the gospel with, because you're not sure how they'll respond, but remember, the gospel saved the demoniac, it saved Paul, and it's powerful enough to help you overcome your fears.

Jesus promised to be with you in this great task. He will be with you when you talk about him with non-Christians. He'll help you if you don't know what to say. He will see your efforts, the Spirit will open their hearts, and he will draw people to himself.

Be encouraged: Jesus does not expect perfection. We all mess up. We all waste golden opportunities to talk about Christ. Or we say the wrong thing. Or we think of something later that we should've said. Or we even avoid a chance to share the gospel. Thankfully, the Lord is gracious, and the gospel is powerful. That grace and that power should motivate us to speak.

Sharing the gospel is a surefire way to make your life count for something—eternally. Not just this life, but forever. You want to build a rock-star reputation in heaven? Then start engaging in gospel business, and get ready to hear, "Well done, good servant."

Conclusion

Into the Deep

Therefore, my beloved brothers, be steadfast, im-
movable, always abounding in the work of the Lord,
knowing that in the Lord your labor is not in vain.

1 Corinthians 15:58

My wife, Jane, and I once had the privilege of scuba diving the
Barrier Reef in the Grand Cayman Islands. The beauty was
staggering. Once we reached a depth of sixty feet, we began
meandering our way through caverns of beautiful coral while
simultaneously coming into schools of massive grouper. Seeing
them from a distance, we thought these huge fish were actually
sharks. Thankfully, we were wrong. At last we arrived at "the
North Wall," where the reef drops off into a huge dark blue
hole. The optical illusion was that there was no bottom to the
ocean. I had never experienced anything like this before. We had

the sensation that we were falling down into this hole, causing us to panic and try to grab the coral around us.

Building a gospel-centered life is like scuba diving. You can either meander through the shallow coral, or you can head for the deep spots and never touch bottom. Let me encourage you to spend the rest of your life diving into the deep. There are riches to find there, even if it takes some work to find them.

This book has focused on helping you learn how to dive, and giving you some gear to help you go deeper. These fourteen chapters and topics are some of the most important for your life, but it's not exhaustive. There's always more, but understanding these principles will allow you to continue to go deeper and grow in grace. As you grow in Christ, you must keep excelling, adding to your walk with him year after year. These chapters have only scraped the surface of what it means to live wisely. It's up to you now to relentlessly apply these truths to yourself.

Take heart in this challenge. Peter gave us reason to take courage when he told us that God has given us everything we need to pursue a life that honors God.[1] The foundation of this kind of wise, gospel-centered life is properly fearing God and putting your faith in Jesus. After that, Peter says, we are to add to our faith virtue, knowledge, self-control, steadfastness, godliness, brotherly affection, and love. Clearly, there's still work to do, there are depths to explore and discover.

Our lives are always in progress. We could carry around a sign that says: "Excuse the Mess: Under Construction." Make your decision now to keep improving. Don't procrastinate on forming good habits. Those habits and patterns of life will become well-worn paths of righteousness for you to follow and for others who will follow after you. If you will embrace the pursuit of wisdom, if you will embrace Jesus, then you will be on the right path.

Just finishing this book isn't enough. You've got to keep growing, keep learning. Live intentionally, disdain mediocrity, and keep your focus on Christ, who is the wisdom of God.

> Get wisdom, and whatever you get, get insight. Prize
>   her highly,
> and she will exalt you; she will honor you if you em-
>   brace her.
>   Proverbs 4:7–8

Notes

Chapter 1: Fear God

1. Proverbs 29:25; Matthew 6:1
2. Proverbs 9:10
3. Proverbs 1:7
4. John 17:17
5. Ecclesiastes 12:13
6. 1 John 2:4

Chapter 2: Know the Bible and Pray Like Crazy

1. 1 Timothy 4:7–8
2. If you want to know more about all the spiritual disciplines, I recommend you read Donald Whitney's book *Spiritual Disciplines for the Christian Life* (Colorado Springs: NavPress, 1991, 2014).
3. 1 Thessalonians 5:17
4. John Piper, "Put in the Fire for the Sake of Prayer," Desiring God, December 28, 2008, http://www.desiringgod.org/sermons/put-in-the-fire-for-the-sake-of-prayer.

Chapter 3: Love the Church

1. Acts 20:28
2. Matthew 16:18
3. 1 Timothy 3:15
4. Charles Spurgeon, "The Best Donation" (No. 2234), an exposition of 2 Corinthians 8:5 delivered on April 5, 1891, at the Metropolitan Tabernacle in London, England.

5. Mark Dever, *Nine Marks of a Healthy Church,* New Expanded Edition (Wheaton, IL: Crossway Books, 2004), 39.

6. Not everything in this passage is meant to be repeatable. This is a description of the early church, not a command for how we should do church today. But since it is a picture of the church body when the apostles were still around, it is a great example and a helpful guide for what a church should look like.

7. John 8:31

Chapter 4: Submit to Authority

1. Romans 12:3

2. John 5:19: "So Jesus said to them, 'Truly, truly, I say to you, the Son can do nothing of his own accord, but only what he sees the Father doing. For whatever the Father does, that the Son does likewise.'"

3. Proverbs 3:2

4. Ephesians 6:1–3

5. 1 Timothy 2:1–2: "First of all, then, I urge that supplications, prayers, intercessions, and thanksgivings be made for all people, for kings and all who are in high positions, that we may lead a peaceful and quiet life, godly and dignified in every way."

6. Hebrews 13:17

Chapter 5: Serve Others

1. David Brooks, *The Road to Character* (New York: Random House, 2015), 6.

2. As quoted in Dave Kindred, *Sound and Fury: Two Powerful Lives, One Fateful Friendship* (New York: Free Press, 2007), 58.

3. Interesting fact: In 1991, I took the opportunity to speak with Muhammad Ali in LaGuardia Airport in New York City. His handlers left him to get dinner, and I moved in to share the gospel with him. He returned the favor and autographed a Muslim tract, and let me know, with those monster hands, he was right.

4. Tyler Kingkade, "Ebola Doctor Kent Brantly Tells Grads Why He Didn't Feel Like a Failure When He Lost Patients," Huffington Post, May 9, 2015, http://www.huffingtonpost.com/2015/05/09/kent-brantly-commencement-speech_n_7249882.html.

5. Mark 10:45

6. Philippians 2:8

Chapter 6: Seek Mentors

1. 2 Corinthians 3:2–3

2. Luke 9:23

Chapter 7: Choose Friends Wisely

1. 1 Corinthians 15:33 NASB

2. Proverbs 13:20

3. Proverbs 17:17
4. Psalm 23:4
5. Philippians 2:20
6. Philippians 2:3–4

Chapter 8: Take More Risks

1. Owen Strachan, *Risky Gospel: Abandon Fear and Build Something Awesome* (Nashville: Nelson, 2013), 32.

Chapter 9: Work Hard

1. Ephesians 5:16
2. Genesis 3:19
3. 1 Corinthians 10:31

Chapter 10: Make Character King

1. "For by grace you have been saved through faith. And this is not your own doing; it is the gift of God, not a result of works, so that no one may boast."
2. Philippians 1:6
3. Job 1:1–5
4. 1 Timothy 4:15
5. 1 John 1:9

Chapter 11: Flee Sexual Immorality

1. This is especially true in Proverbs 1–9.
2. Proverbs 5:3–6
3. Proverbs uses a lot of personification, where something that isn't a person (like wisdom or foolishness) is referred to like it is a person (i.e., Lady Wisdom). Here, the author refers to sexual temptation as a woman.
4. Proverbs 5:8
5. Proverbs 5:12–13
6. Romans 13:14

Chapter 12: Embrace Correction

1. Ecclesiastes 7:5
2. Proverbs 27:6
3. Hebrews 4:12
4. James 4:17

Chapter 13: Know the Gospel

1. The Silk Road was an old collection of routes people used to connect places like Europe, China, and India. It allowed the countries to trade and travel.
2. 1 Timothy 1:15

3. Romans 3:23
4. Romans 5:12
5. 2 Corinthians 5:21
6. 2 Corinthians 5:17

Chapter 14: Speak, Defend, and Spread the Gospel

1. 1 Corinthians 1:26-31
2. 2 Corinthians 5:20
3. Jude 1:3
4. 1 Peter 3:15
5. Colossians 4:5–6

Conclusion: Into the Deep

1. 2 Peter 1:3–11

Dan Dumas has served as a college pastor for fourteen years with extensive experience discipling young people. Dan serves as a senior vice president at The Southern Baptist Theological Seminary, where he teaches and provides leadership for youth conferences (RENOWN and D3). He also teaches classes at Boyce College. Dan lives with his wife and children in Louis-ville, Kentucky.

Continue the conversation . . .
Blog: dandumas.com
Twitter: @DanDumas
Facebook
Pinterest: www.pinterest.com/dandumas